Math Fun Grade 3

Best Value Books

Table of Contents

WESTERN EDUCATIONAL ACTIVITIES LTD.
12006 - 111 Ave. Edmonton, Alberta T5G 0E6
Ph: (780) 413-7055   Fax: (780) 413-7056
GST # R105636187

The student pages in this book have been specially prepared for reproduction on any standard copying machine.

Kelley Wingate products are available at fine educational supply stores throughout the U.S. and Canada.

Math Fun Grade 3 **CD-3723**   Printed in the United States of America   ISBN 0-88724-441-6

About the book...

This book is just one in our Best Value™ series of reproducible, skill oriented activity books. Each book is developmentally appropriate and contains over 100 pages packed with educationally sound classroom-tested activities. Each book also contains free skill cards and resource pages filled with extended activity ideas.

The activities in this book have been developed to help students master the basic skills necessary to succeed in mathematics. The activities have been sequenced to help insure successful completion of the assigned tasks, thus building positive self-esteem as well as the self-confidence students need to meet academic and social challenges.

The activities may be used by themselves, as supplemental activities, or as enrichment material for the mathematics program.

Developed by teachers and tested by students, we never lost sight of the fact that if students don't stay motivated and involved, they will never truly grasp the skills being taught on a cognitive level.

About the author...

Dawn Talluto Jacobi holds a Bachelor's degree in Mathematics. While raising her three children (Eric, Kaitlin, and Matthew) Dawn found herself in demand as math tutor. She noted a common thread that kept children from finding success in math class - the lack of self-confidence. Dawn developed a game format that attracted and held her students' attention because it made math more fun. Dawn discovered that she enjoyed teaching and decided to enter the field full time. She is currently teaching high school Algebra and is working on her Master's degree in Education.

Senior Editors: Patricia Pedigo and Dr. Roger De Santi
Production Director: Homer Desrochers
Production: Debra Ollier

Ready-To-Use Ideas and Activities

The activities in this book will help children master the basic skills necessary to become competent learners. Remember, as you read through the activities listed below and as you go through this book, that all children learn at their own rate. Although repetition is important, it is critical that we never lose sight of the fact that it is equally important to build children's self-esteem and self-confidence if we want them to become successful learners.

Flashcard ideas

The back of this book has removable flash cards that will be great for basic skill and enrichment activities. Pull the flash cards out and cut them apart (if you have access to a paper cutter, use that). Following are several ideas for use of the flash cards.

- Use the flash cards to practice and reinforce multiplication and division facts. Always remember to tell students the number of problems that were answered correctly. For example, if the student answers 8 problems correctly out of ten, tell the student that he or she got 8 problems correct, not "you missed three". Building self-confidence and fostering good feelings about learning is very important.

- Give each child three or four flash cards. Call out number sentences and have students hold up the correct answer card.

- Turn the flash cards with the number sentence showing. Have students match equivalent number sentences. Self-check by looking at the answers on the back of the card.

- Play team "High-Low". Divide the cards into two piles. Two students turn over the top two cards and answer the number sentence. The player with the highest answer takes both cards. Pass the pile on to the next student and repeat. The team with the most cards at the end wins.

i

Ready-To-Use Ideas and Activities

Multiplication Bee

Try this twist to a classroom favorite. Using the flash cards in the back of this book, stack all of the multiplication cards in a deck with the problem facing up. Line all students up and ask the first student to answer a multiplication problem. if the student answers it correctly, then he or she remains standing. Students that do not answer correctly, return to their desks. The student left standing is the winner.

Multiplication Race

Divide students into three groups. Have each group line up. Using the flash cards in the back of this book, stack all of the multiplication cards in a deck with the problem facing up. Ask the first person in each group to walk to the chalkboard and write the answer to a problem that you call out, if the answer is correct, that group receives a point. The group with the most points at the end of the game wins.

Reproduce the bingo sheet included in this book, making enough to have one for each student. Hand them out to the students. Take the flash cards and write the problems on the chalk board. Have the students choose 24 of the problems and write them in any order on the empty spaces of their bingo cards, writing only one problem in each space. When all students have finished filling out their bingo cards, take the flash cards and make them in to a deck. Call out the answers one at a time. Any student who has a problem that equals the called out answer should make an "X" through the problem to cross it out. The student who crosses out five problems in a row first (horizontally, vertically, or diagonally) wins the game and shouts "BINGO!". Another fun version of this game is to write answers on the bingo cards and call out the problems. To extend the game you can continue playing until you a student crosses out all of the problems on his bingo sheet.

Challenge your own score! The next two pages include basic addition and subtraction problems which children should memorize. To help them we suggest you make multiple copies of these pages. Work on only one page at a time. Get a minute timer. See how many problems the child can do correctly in one minute. Record the child's score on a piece of paper. Let the child try again and see how many problems he/she can do correctly. The more times a child does each page, the higher his/her score will become and the more problems he/she will learn. As scores increase so does a child's self-confidence.

Name _____   Date _____

1.
$3\overline{)27}$

2.
$2\overline{)6}$

3.
$5\overline{)15}$

4.
$3\overline{)12}$

5.
$8\overline{)24}$

6.
$9\overline{)45}$

7.
$8\overline{)48}$

8.
$4\overline{)16}$

9.
$2\overline{)10}$

10.
$7\overline{)42}$

11.
$9\overline{)72}$

12.
$4\overline{)28}$

13.
$2\overline{)14}$

14.
$5\overline{)25}$

15.
$6\overline{)42}$

16.
$7\overline{)63}$

17.
$8\overline{)64}$

18.
$5\overline{)20}$

19.
$2\overline{)8}$

20.
$5\overline{)10}$

21.
$8\overline{)40}$

22.
$9\overline{)36}$

23.
$2\overline{)12}$

24.
$3\overline{)21}$

25.
$4\overline{)32}$

26.
$7\overline{)35}$

27.
$6\overline{)30}$

28.
$4\overline{)20}$

29.
$9\overline{)54}$

30.
$7\overline{)28}$

31.
$9\overline{)18}$

32.
$6\overline{)18}$

33.
$4\overline{)8}$

34.
$7\overline{)49}$

35.
$5\overline{)35}$

36.
$3\overline{)24}$

37.
$2\overline{)18}$

38.
$5\overline{)45}$

39.
$9\overline{)81}$

40.
$5\overline{)15}$

41.
$7\overline{)14}$

42.
$4\overline{)12}$

43.
$3\overline{)9}$

44.
$4\overline{)36}$

45.
$6\overline{)36}$

46.
$8\overline{)56}$

47.
$6\overline{)12}$

48.
$9\overline{)63}$

49.
$8\overline{)72}$

50.
$5\overline{)40}$

51.
$9\overline{)27}$

52.
$6\overline{)48}$

53.
$8\overline{)16}$

54.
$4\overline{)24}$

55.
$3\overline{)6}$

56.
$8\overline{)32}$

57.
$6\overline{)54}$

58.
$7\overline{)56}$

59.
$5\overline{)30}$

60.
$2\overline{)16}$

61.
$3\overline{)18}$

62.
$6\overline{)24}$

63.
$7\overline{)21}$

64.
$2\overline{)4}$

65.
$6\overline{)30}$

66.
$8\overline{)16}$

67.
$2\overline{)10}$

68.
$3\overline{)24}$

69.
$9\overline{)45}$

70.
$4\overline{)12}$

71.
$7\overline{)49}$

72.
$5\overline{)45}$

                   CD-3723

Name _____   Date_____

1.	1 x 1	2.	3 x 9	3.	4 x 1	4.	7 x 2	5.	1 x 3	6.	4 x 2	7.	7 x 3	8.	4 x 5

9. 6 x 8   10. 2 x 0   11. 1 x 2   12. 1 x 7   13. 8 x 4   14. 7 x 5   15. 2 x 3   16. 4 x 4

17. 7 x 1   18. 1 x 8   19. 2 x 2   20. 4 x 3   21. 2 x 6   22. 6 x 7   23. 1 x 4   24. 7 x 4

25. 6 x 9   26. 1 x 6   27. 7 x 6   28. 9 x 0   29. 2 x 1   30. 1 x 5   31. 6 x 6   32. 3 x 8

33. 5 x 6   34. 1 x 0   35. 2 x 8   36. 3 x 4   37. 4 x 0   38. 1 x 9   39. 6 x 4   40. 7 x 7

41. 6 x 1   42. 2 x 5   43. 7 x 8   44. 5 x 5   45. 2 x 4   46. 3 x 6   47. 5 x 0   48. 5 x 4

49. 3 x 3   50. 4 x 8   51. 7 x 9   52. 4 x 9   53. 5 x 8   54. 5 x 3   55. 6 x 5   56. 2 x 7

57. 5 x 2   58. 5 x 7   59. 2 x 9   60. 9 x 1   61. 6 x 3   62. 4 x 7   63. 7 x 0   64. 5 x 9

65. 6 x 2   66. 5 x 1   67. 3 x 7   68. 8 x 3   69. 4 x 6   70. 6 x 3   71. 8 x 1   72. 8 x 2

iv   CD-3723

Reproduce this page and make your own math bingo game! Use in conjunction with the enclosed flash cards. Popular formats: caller calls equation and students mark answers or caller calls answers and students mark correct equations.

B I N G O

		Free!		

v

CD-3723

Hundreds Chart

1	2	3	4	5	6	7	8	9	10
11	12	13	14	15	16	17	18	19	20
21	22	23	24	25	26	27	28	29	30
31	32	33	34	35	36	37	38	39	40
41	42	43	44	45	46	47	48	49	50
51	52	53	54	55	56	57	58	59	60
61	62	63	64	65	66	67	68	69	70
71	72	73	74	75	76	77	78	79	80
81	82	83	84	85	86	87	88	89	90
91	92	93	94	95	96	97	98	99	100

Multiplication and Division Table

x /÷	1	2	3	4	5	6	7	8	9
1	1	2	3	4	5	6	7	8	9
2	2	4	6	8	10	12	14	16	18
3	3	6	9	12	15	18	21	24	27
4	4	8	12	16	20	24	28	32	36
5	5	10	15	20	25	30	35	40	45
6	6	12	18	24	30	36	42	48	54
7	7	14	21	28	35	42	49	56	63
8	8	16	24	32	40	48	56	64	72
9	9	18	27	36	45	54	63	72	81

Hopscotch

Use your math facts to complete the hopscotch board.

1. 3 + 2 =   - 4 =   + 9 =

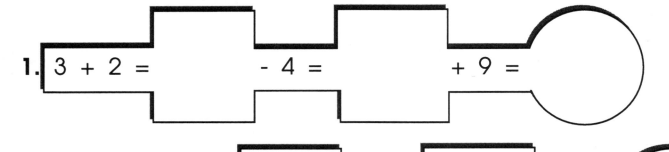

2. 8 + 1 =   - 2 =   + 4 =

3. 4 + 1 =   + 8 =   - 5 =

4. 7 + 2 =   - 1 =   + 4 =

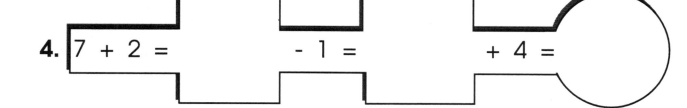

5. 3 + 8 =   - 2 =   + 4 =

6. 6 + 1 =   + 5 =   - 4 =

Hopscotch

Use your math facts to complete the hopscotch board.

1. $7 + 7 =$ $- 5 =$ $+ 3 =$

2. $3 + 4 =$ $+ 5 =$ $- 8 =$

3. $16 - 9 =$ $+ 4 =$ $- 6 =$

4. $3 + 9 =$ $- 8 =$ $+ 9 =$

5. $6 + 8 =$ $- 9 =$ $+ 8 =$

6. $15 - 8 =$ $+ 5 =$ $- 6 =$

CD-3723

Hopscotch

Use your math facts to complete the hopscotch board.

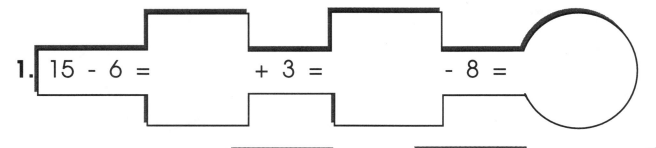

1. 15 - 6 =   + 3 =   - 8 =

2. 13 - 8 =   + 6 =   - 9 =

3. 8 + 6 =   - 7 =   + 5 =

4. 7 + 9 =   - 8 =   + 3 =

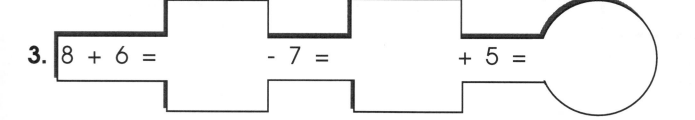

5. 12 - 8 =   + 7 =   - 5 =

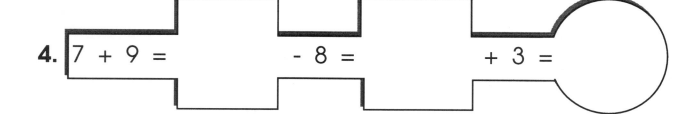

6. 18 - 9 =   + 5 =   - 7 =

Name_____

Hopscotch

Use your math facts to complete the hopscotch board.

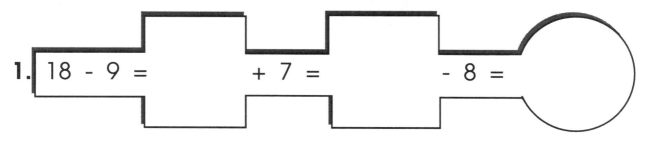

1. 18 - 9 =   + 7 =   - 8 =

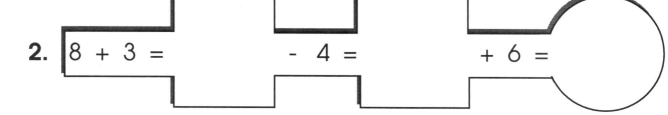

2. 8 + 3 =   - 4 =   + 6 =

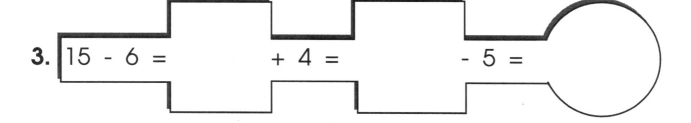

3. 15 - 6 =   + 4 =   - 5 =

4. 6 + 5 =   - 8 =   + 6 =

5. 5 + 9 =   - 6 =   + 9 =

6. 17 - 9 =   + 5 =   - 7 =

         CD-3723

Compare Squares

Compare the number sentences. Write <, >, or = in the square to make a true math statement. The first problem is done for you.

1. 3 + 6 $\boxed{<}$ 7 + 4

11. 15 - 7 $\square$ 13 - 8

2. 18 - 9 $\square$ 13 - 5

12. 5 + 9 $\square$ 6 + 7

3. 5 + 8 $\square$ 9 + 6

13. 7 + 9 $\square$ 8 + 9

4. 13 - 4 $\square$ 12 - 3

14. 12 - 4 $\square$ 8 + 4

5. 6 + 6 $\square$ 9 + 2

15. 7 + 5 $\square$ 15 - 6

6. 16 - 8 $\square$ 11 - 2

16. 18 - 9 $\square$ 6 + 5

7. 7 + 8 $\square$ 9 + 5

17. 5 + 9 $\square$ 8 + 8

8. 15 - 9 $\square$ 12 - 5

18. 17 - 9 $\square$ 3 + 6

9. 14 - 6 $\square$ 11 - 4

19. 8 + 7 $\square$ 9 + 5

10. 7 + 6 $\square$ 4 + 9

20. 13 - 6 $\square$ 6 + 4

Compare Squares

Compare the number sentences. Write >, <, or = in the square to make a true math statement. The first problem is done for you.

1. 6 + 4 [<] 9 + 2

2. 14 - 8 [ ] 17 - 9

3. 8 + 5 [ ] 9 + 6

4. 7 + 4 [ ] 6 + 5

5. 6 + 8 [ ] 9 + 4

6. 12 - 3 [ ] 14 - 6

7. 7 + 9 [ ] 8 + 8

8. 15 - 7 [ ] 16 - 9

9. 14 - 7 [ ] 12 - 4

10. 13 - 5 [ ] 17 - 9

11. 6 + 6 [ ] 9 + 2

12. 16 - 7 [ ] 12 - 5

13. 3 + 8 [ ] 9 + 4

14. 16 - 8 [ ] 6 + 3

15. 17 - 8 [ ] 8 + 2

16. 4 + 8 [ ] 6 + 6

17. 12 - 9 [ ] 13 - 5

18. 8 + 9 [ ] 6 + 7

19. 13 - 7 [ ] 4 + 4

20. 8 + 7 [ ] 16 - 9

Compare Squares

Compare the number sentences. Write <, >, or = in the square to make a true math statement. The first problem is done for you.

1. $3 + 7 - 5$ $\boxed{<}$ $2 + 2 + 2$

11. $9 + 4 - 5$ $\square$ $15 - 6 + 2$

2. $18 - 9 + 3$ $\square$ $5 + 8 - 4$

12. $13 - 6 + 4$ $\square$ $5 + 4 + 3$

3. $4 + 8 - 3$ $\square$ $17 - 9 + 2$

13. $15 - 6 - 2$ $\square$ $4 + 6 - 3$

4. $12 - 4 + 6$ $\square$ $9 + 6 - 8$

14. $9 + 2 - 5$ $\square$ $8 - 4 + 5$

5. $4 + 5 + 6$ $\square$ $3 + 6 + 5$

15. $7 + 5 - 6$ $\square$ $3 + 3 - 0$

6. $11 - 4 - 3$ $\square$ $8 + 3 - 6$

16. $14 - 6 + 3$ $\square$ $9 + 5 - 4$

7. $5 + 3 + 8$ $\square$ $12 - 4 + 9$

17. $12 - 9 + 7$ $\square$ $17 - 9 + 2$

8. $14 - 6 + 2$ $\square$ $11 - 8 + 7$

18. $8 + 1 - 4$ $\square$ $15 - 7 + 1$

9. $3 + 8 - 6$ $\square$ $2 + 7 - 3$

19. $3 + 7 + 7$ $\square$ $4 + 8 + 6$

10. $15 - 8 + 4$ $\square$ $2 + 4 + 6$

20. $3 + 4 - 2$ $\square$ $6 + 3 - 4$

 CD-3723

Compare Squares

Compare the number sentences. Write <, >, or = in the square to make a true math statement. The first problem is done for you.

1. 5 + 8 - 4 $\boxed{<}$ 13 - 6 + 3   **11.** 14 - 5 + 8 ☐ 16 - 9 + 7

2. 15 - 6 - 5 ☐ 18 - 9 - 8   **12.** 5 + 7 - 4 ☐ 8 + 6 - 7

3. 4 + 8 + 3 ☐ 12 - 6 + 8   **13.** 15 - 8 - 6 ☐ 13 - 5 + 8

4. 12 - 7 - 1 ☐ 5 + 6 - 4   **14.** 5 + 4 + 8 ☐ 2 + 6 + 9

5. 13 - 6 + 7 ☐ 7 + 2 + 3   **15.** 16 - 9 + 4 ☐ 12 - 4 + 5

6. 8 + 5 - 4 ☐ 15 - 6 + 3   **16.** 16 - 7 + 4 ☐ 7 + 5 - 3

7. 9 + 8 - 7 ☐ 8 + 4 - 3   **17.** 16 - 9 + 5 ☐ 13 - 5 + 4

8. 16 - 8 + 7 ☐ 7 + 2 + 9   **18.** 18 - 9 - 6 ☐ 15 - 7 - 4

9. 12 - 9 + 8 ☐ 15 - 9 + 6   **19.** 5 + 7 + 5 ☐ 4 + 5 + 9

10. 4 + 4 + 4 ☐ 5 + 8 - 4   **20.** 13 - 8 + 5 ☐ 8 + 6 - 3

Leapfrog

Use your math facts to move across the lily pads.

1. 3 + 6 = ⬭ - 4 = ⬭

2. 7 + 8 = ⬭ - 9 = ⬭

3. 17 - 9 = ⬭ + 8 = ⬭

4. 9 + 3 = ⬭ - 6 = ⬭

5. 14 - 8 = ⬭ + 7 = ⬭

6. 12 - 3 = ⬭ + 4 = ⬭

7. 5 + 6 = ⬭ -7 = ⬭

8. 15 - 7 = ⬭ + 3 = ⬭

9. 7 + 9 = ⬭ - 8 = ⬭

10. 13 - 5 = ⬭ + 9 = ⬭

Bonus

$$16 - 8 = \boxed{}$$

$$+ 9 = \boxed{}$$

$$+ 1 = \boxed{}$$

Leapfrog

Use your math facts to move across the lily pads.

1. 12 - 6 = + 4 =

2. 15 - 9 = + 8 =

3. 9 + 4 = - 6 =

4. 11 - 3 = + 7 =

5. 14 - 8 = + 9 =

6. 7 + 7 = - 5 =

7. 5 + 8 = - 4 =

8. 12 - 5 = + 8 =

9. 2 + 9 = - 4 =

10. 13 - 4 = + 9 =

Bonus

$$6 + 7$$

$$- 8$$

$$+ 9$$

CD-3723

Blankety- Blanks

Solve the problems below and write the answer in the box. On the blanket,
shade in all the numbers that are in the answer boxes.
The answers will make a pattern.

$5 + 7 - 4 = \Box$

$5 + 5 - 7 = \Box$

$4 + 5 + 9 = \Box$

$2 + 7 - 8 = \Box$

$4 + 7 - 5 = \Box$

$15 - 8 + 3 = \Box$

$12 - 3 + 8 = \Box$

$5 + 9 - 7 = \Box$

$8 + 8 - 7 = \Box$

$14 - 9 + 8 = \Box$

$9 + 3 - 7 = \Box$

$14 - 9 + 7 = \Box$

$10 - 3 + 8 = \Box$

$13 - 9 + 7 = \Box$

$2 + 6 + 8 = \Box$

$15 - 8 + 7 = \Box$

11	3	13	18
0	4	7	19
14	21	20	25
21	23	5	4
17	19	30	0
20	27	9	21
16	2	31	26
33	0	6	19
12	24	22	20
1	10	15	8

Blankety- Blanks

Solve the problems below and write the answer in the box. On the blanket, shade in all the numbers that are in the answer boxes.
The answers will make a pattern.

$4 + 7 - 5 =$ ☐

$15 - 6 + 8 =$ ☐

$3 + 4 + 9 =$ ☐

$18 - 9 + 3 =$ ☐

$15 - 9 + 2 =$ ☐

$14 - 7 + 4 =$ ☐

$16 - 8 + 7 =$ ☐

$7 + 8 - 6 =$ ☐

$12 - 3 + 9 =$ ☐

$11 - 4 + 3 =$ ☐

$13 - 5 - 4 =$ ☐

$17 - 9 + 5 =$ ☐

$7 + 6 - 8 =$ ☐

$16 - 7 + 5 =$ ☐

$3 + 8 - 4 =$ ☐

$14 - 5 - 6 =$ ☐

11	0	19	6
3	23	30	8
24	21	20	25
23	15	16	34
2	17	7	0
20	9	5	21
30	14	10	26
33	0	31	19
12	24	22	13
18	1	20	4

Name _____

Regrouping

Add the following problems. Do not forget to regroup when necessary.

52	36	85	17	43	36	25	49
+ 19	+ 84	+ 46	+ 55	+ 29	+ 38	+ 68	+19

59	22	46	23	55	65	79	44
+ 28	+ 57	+ 39	+ 37	+ 28	+ 26	+ 17	+ 27

53	36	26	37	48	39	69	47
+ 38	+ 39	+ 47	+ 44	+ 19	+ 28	+ 22	+ 24

77	38	56	27	45	29	53	37
+ 16	+ 58	+ 29	+ 37	+ 38	+ 61	+ 29	+ 28

48 + 23 =   26 + 39 =   46 + 27 =   36 + 16 =

46 + 35 =   77 + 15 =   48 + 27 =   17 + 54 =

38 + 38 =   52 + 29 =   35 + 27 =   44 + 36 =

61 + 29 =   36 + 46 =   34 + 28 =   53 + 27 =

68 + 28 =   47 + 23 =   67 + 29 =   39 + 48 =

 CD-3723

Regrouping

Add the following problems. Do not forget to regroup when necessary.

17	28	55	34	57	38	24
+ 75	+ 37	+ 19	+ 46	+ 33	+ 45	+ 46

79	34	35	65	55	64	49
+ 22	+ 77	+ 67	+ 48	+ 78	+ 66	+ 62

452	243	786	689	576	779	389
+ 238	+ 139	+ 145	+ 149	+ 235	+ 160	+ 421

570	223	696	338	589	248	199
+ 145	+ 499	+ 216	+ 377	+ 147	+ 388	+ 559

69 + 53 =   27 + 85 =   49 + 71 =

35 + 66 =   36 + 89 =   55 + 45 =

48 + 92 =   77 + 34 =   96 + 38 =

57 + 49 =   85 + 77 =   60 + 82 =

193 + 268 =   284 + 346 =   356 + 475 =

     CD-3723

Regrouping

Add the following problems. Do not forget to regroup when necessary.

3,123	3,142	6,522	4,657	3,826
+ 4,938	+ 3,859	+ 1,479	+ 1,393	+ 4,575

5,777	3,575	6,259	2,474	7,389
+ 2,633	+ 2,437	+ 1,853	+ 2,787	+ 1,622

2,842	5,486	3,389	4,576	3,974
+ 1,658	+ 1,526	+ 4,949	+ 1,545	+ 4,148

3,773	2,196	6,438	5,719	2,399
+ 1,648	+ 3,916	+ 2,777	+ 1,284	+ 2,139

1,269 + 4,153 =   2,427 + 5,285 =

3,179 + 1,471 =   3,235 + 2,966 =

5,436 + 1,589 =   4,556 + 2,458 =

6,358 + 1,942 =   4,377 + 2,624 =

2,845 + 1,676 =   3,156 + 4,855 =

Regrouping

Subtract the following problems. Do not forget to regroup when necessary.

40	38	42	87	74	93	84	66
- 29	- 19	- 16	- 39	- 15	- 74	- 35	- 48

52	46	72	61	67	54	92	75
- 24	- 28	- 53	- 28	- 38	- 36	- 73	- 28

58	53	81	92	71	71	93	54
- 39	- 29	- 32	- 59	- 64	- 32	- 76	- 39

73	95	84	64	83	43	52	81
- 25	- 48	- 27	- 39	- 28	- 34	- 47	- 27

47 - 18 =   41 - 25 =   84 - 47 =   75 - 46 =

86 - 39 =   55 - 17 =   61 - 12 =   71 - 34 =

34 - 18 =   62 - 49 =   75 - 17 =   43 - 38 =

73 - 38 =   94 - 66 =   86 - 58 =   56 - 49 =

44 - 15 =   42 - 28 =   96 - 29 =   91 - 56 =

Regrouping

Subtract the following problems. Do not forget to regroup when necessary.

326	972	438	371	407	738	954
- 285	- 689	- 259	- 296	- 138	- 199	- 466

529	514	625	560	522	464	743
- 262	- 407	- 467	- 382	- 278	- 267	- 166

632	643	586	257	416	371	814
- 238	- 439	- 197	- 149	- 187	- 184	- 465

774	323	486	634	811	635	642
- 189	- 199	- 397	- 277	- 347	- 498	- 299

222 - 153 =   423 - 285 =   843 - 477 =

435 - 166 =   536 - 189 =   415 - 248 =

628 - 199 =   317 - 128 =   347 - 188 =

757 - 179 =   632 - 377 =   431 - 382 =

673 - 388 =   754 - 686 =   956 - 587 =

Regrouping

Subtract the following problems. Do not forget to regroup when necessary.

3,246 - 2,685	4,318 - 2,529	3,741 - 2,962	7,358 - 1,979	9,534 - 4,696
5,269 - 2,682	6,125 - 3,467	5,622 - 3,826	4,264 - 2,678	7,143 - 1,667
4,632 - 2,938	5,386 - 1,497	2,537 - 1,849	3,171 - 1,284	8,514 - 4,865
7,732 - 6,984	4,386 - 3,977	6,234 - 4,277	6,351 - 4,498	6,742 - 2,995

2,422 - 1,543 =   6,423 - 3,585 =

8,436 - 4,778 =   4,135 - 1,647 =

5,362 - 4,969 =   3,415 - 2,548 =

6,728 - 1,999 =   3,127 - 1,288 =

3,347 - 1,688 =   5,123 - 3,694 =

   CD-3723

Regrouping

Subtract the following problems. Do not forget to regroup when necessary.

30	70	80	70	40	70	60	80
- 17	- 49	- 59	- 46	- 32	- 31	- 27	- 59

50	40	60	60	50	60	90	70
- 34	- 29	- 48	- 18	- 38	- 56	- 57	- 28

60	50	80	90	70	70	90	50
- 28	- 44	- 65	- 59	- 17	- 52	- 71	- 29

70	90	80	60	80	40	50	30
- 35	- 88	- 23	- 28	- 57	- 32	- 48	- 12

20 - 18 =   40 - 25 =   80 - 47 =   70 - 46 =

80 - 39 =   50 - 17 =   60 - 12 =   70 - 34 =

30 - 18 =   60 - 49 =   70 - 17 =   40 - 38 =

70 - 38 =   90 - 66 =   80 - 58 =   50 - 49 =

40 - 15 =   40 - 28 =   90 - 29 =   90 - 56 =

19   CD-3723

Regrouping

Subtract the following problems. Do not forget to regroup when necessary.

306	970	408	300	407	730	900
- 214	- 389	- 159	- 196	- 125	- 506	- 466

509	510	605	500	520	404	700
- 352	- 287	- 582	- 356	- 288	- 367	- 546

602	640	506	200	410	801	800
- 136	- 479	- 192	- 123	- 381	- 354	- 645

707	120	406	600	810	605	600
- 529	- 106	- 179	- 257	- 446	- 528	- 328

202 - 135 =   420 - 258 =   800 - 367 =

405 - 116 =   530 - 198 =   400 - 284 =

608 - 149 =   310 - 182 =   300 - 125 =

707 - 198 =   630 - 458 =   400 - 328 =

603 - 324 =   750 - 268 =   900 - 578 =

Name _____

Regrouping

Subtract the following problems. Do not forget to regroup when necessary.

3,540	6,307	3,041	7,300	9,000
- 2,865	- 2,639	- 2,692	- 4,897	- 4,569

5,260	6,105	5,022	4,200	7,000
- 3,852	- 4,479	- 3,745	- 1,522	- 4,523

4,630	5,306	2,037	3,100	8,000
- 3,841	- 2,827	- 1,958	- 2,247	- 5,724

7,730	4,306	6,034	6,300	6,000
- 3,852	- 1,977	- 2,699	- 1,432	- 5,116

2,420 - 1,683 =   6,203 - 4,384 =

9,200 - 7,746 =   4,000 - 2,674 =

5,630 - 4,652 =   3,504 - 2,845 =

6,700 - 3,611 =   3,000 - 1,828 =

4,330 - 1,841 =   7,100 - 3,546 =

Name _____

Beat the Clock

How quickly can you complete this page? Time yourself. Ready, set, go!

Time : _____

Number Correct : _____

2 x 3	2 x 1	2 x 11	2 x 8	2 x 0	2 x 5	2 x 2	2 x 10

2 x 7	2 x 4	2 x 9	2 x 12	2 x 6	2 x 4	2 x 1	2 x 3

6 x 2	7 x 2	3 x 2	2 x 2	8 x 2	11 x 2	0 x 2	1 x 2

9 x 2	12 x 2	5 x 2	6 x 2	10 x 2	4 x 2	7 x 2	3 x 2

9 x 2 =	7 x 2 =	4 x 2 =	3 x 2 =	6 x 2 =
5 x 2 =	8 x 2 =	7 x 2 =	9 x 2 =	2 x 2 =
0 x 2 =	3 x 2 =	8 x 2 =	5 x 2 =	6 x 2 =
2 x 7 =	2 x 1 =	2 x 5 =	2 x 2 =	2 x 9 =
10 x 2 =	12 x 2 =	11 x 2 =	7 x 2 =	4 x 2 =

       CD-3723

Beat the Clock

How quickly can you complete this page? Time yourself. Ready, set, go!

Time : _____
Number Correct : _____

2 x 3	5 x 3	1 x 3	0 x 3	4 x 3	3 x 3	6 x 3	9 x 3
11 x 3	7 x 3	10 x 3	8 x 3	5 x 3	6 x 3	2 x 3	4 x 3
3 x 5	3 x 4	3 x 3	3 x 9	3 x 11	3 x 1	3 x 6	3 x 10
3 x 2	3 x 12	3 x 0	3 x 7	3 x 8	3 x 4	3 x 3	3 x 9

9 x 3 =   7 x 3 =   4 x 3 =   3 x 3 =   6 x 3 =

5 x 3 =   8 x 3 =   7 x 3 =   9 x 3 =   2 x 3 =

3 x 2 =   3 x 3 =   3 x 8 =   3 x 6 =   3 x 0 =

3 x 4 =   3 x 1 =   3 x 5 =   3 x 9 =   3 x 7 =

10 x 3 =   12 x 3 =   11 x 3 =   4 x 3 =   6 x 3 =

Beat the Clock

How quickly can you complete this page? Time yourself. Ready, set, go!

Time : _____
Number Correct : _____

4	4	4	4	4	4	4	4
x 3	x 5	x 9	x 10	x 0	x 6	x 4	x 7

4	4	4	4	4	4	4	4
x 2	x 8	x 7	x 11	x 1	x 12	x 3	x 9

6	7	3	2	10	4	5	11
x 4	x 4	x 4	x 4	x 4	x 4	x 4	x 4

0	8	9	12	1	4	7	2
x 4	x 4	x 4	x 4	x 4	x 4	x 4	x 4

9 x 4 =   7 x 4 =   4 x 4 =   3 x 4 =   6 x 4 =

5 x 4 =   8 x 4 =   1 x 4 =   0 x 4 =   2 x 4 =

4 x 2 =   4 x 3 =   4 x 8 =   4 x 6 =   4 x 0 =

4 x 4 =   4 x 1 =   4 x 5 =   4 x 7 =   4 x 9 =

10 x 4 =   12 x 4 =   11 x 4 =   4 x 4 =   8 x 4 =

Name _____

Beat the Clock

How quickly can you complete this page? Time yourself. Ready, set, go!

Time : _____
Number Correct : _____

5 x 3	5 x5	5 x 9	5 x 10	5 x 7	5 x 0	5 x 6	5 x 1
5 x 2	5 x8	5 x 4	5 x 11	5 x 1	5 x 12	5 x 3	5 x 5
6 x 5	7 x 5	3 x 5	12 x 5	0 x 5	5 x 5	2 x 5	11 x 5
9 x 5	4 x 5	8 x 5	10 x 5	1 x 5	3 x 5	7 x 5	6 x 5

9 x 5 =   7 x 5 =   4 x 5 =   3 x 5 =   6 x 5 =

5 x 5 =   8 x 5 =   0 x 5 =   1 x 5 =   2 x 5 =

5 x 2 =   5 x 3 =   5 x 8 =   5 x 6 =   5 x 0 =

5 x 4 =   5 x 7 =   5 x 5 =   5 x 9 =   5 x 1 =

10 x 5 =   11 x 5 =   10 x 5 =   7 x 5 =   4 x 5 =

Name _____

Beat the Clock

How quickly can you complete this page? Time yourself. Ready, set, go!

Time : _____
Number Correct : _____

6	6	6	6	6	6	6	6
x 3	x 5	x 9	x 0	x 10	x 7	x 11	x 1

6	6	6	6	6	6	6	6
x 2	x 8	x 12	x 1	x 4	x 6	x 3	x 5

6	7	3	2	11	5	12	1
x 6	x 6	x 6	x 6	x 6	x 6	x 6	x 6

9	8	10	0	1	4	5	3
x 6	x 6	x 6	x 6	x 6	x 6	x 6	x 6

1 x 6 =   7 x 6 =   4 x 6 =   3 x 6 =   6 x 6 =

5 x 6 =   8 x 6 =   0 x 6 =   9 x 6 =   2 x 6 =

6 x 7 =   6 x 3 =   6 x 8 =   6 x 6 =   6 x 0 =

6 x 4 =   6 x 9 =   6 x 5 =   6 x 2 =   6 x 1 =

10 x 6 =   12 x 6 =   11 x 6 =   7 x 6 =   3 x 6 =

Beat the Clock

How quickly can you complete this page? Time yourself. Ready, set, go!

Time : _____
Number Correct : _____

7 x 3	7 x 5	7 x 11	7 x 5	7 x 10	7 x 4	7 x 7	7 x 9
7 x 2	7 x 8	7 x 0	7 x 1	7 x 12	7 x 6	7 x 3	7 x 8
6 x 7	7 x 7	4 x 7	2 x 7	12 x 7	8 x 7	3 x 7	11 x 7
9 x 7	0 x 7	8 x 7	5 x 7	1 x 7	10 x 7	7 x 7	1 x 7

1 x 7 =   7 x 7 =   4 x 7 =   3 x 7 =   6 x 7 =

5 x 7 =   8 x 7 =   0 x 7 =   9 x 7 =   2 x 7 =

7 x 7 =   7 x 3 =   7 x 8 =   7 x 6 =   7 x 0 =

7 x 4 =   7 x 9 =   7 x 5 =   7 x 2 =   7 x 1 =

11 x 7 =   10 x 7 =   12 x 7 =   7 x 7 =   4 x 7 =

Name _____

Beat the Clock

How quickly can you complete this page? Time yourself. Ready, set, go!

Time : _____
Number Correct : _____

8 x 3	8 x 5	8 x 9	8 x 4	8 x 11	8 x 0	8 x 7	8 x 9
8 x 2	8 x 8	8 x 12	8 x 1	8 x 10	8 x 6	8 x 3	8 x 5
10 x 8	5 x 8	12 x 8	2 x 8	3 x 8	7 x 8	6 x 8	0 x 8
9 x 8	11 x 8	8 x 8	6 x 8	1 x 8	4 x 8	5 x 8	7 x 8

5 x 8 =   1 x 8 =   4 x 8 =   3 x 8 =   6 x 8 =

0 x 8 =   8 x 8 =   7 x 8 =   9 x 8 =   2 x 8 =

8 x 9 =   8 x 3 =   8 x 8 =   8 x 6 =   8 x 0 =

8 x 4 =   8 x 7 =   8 x 5 =   8 x 2 =   8 x 1 =

11 x 8 =   10 x 8 =   12 x 8 =   3 x 8 =   9 x 8 =

Name _____

Beat the Clock

How quickly can you complete this page? Time yourself. Ready, set, go!

Time : _____
Number Correct : _____

9	9	9	9	9	9	9	9
x 12	x 10	x 9	x 5	x 3	x 11	x 4	x 0

9	9	9	9	9	9	9	9
x 7	x 8	x 2	x 1	x 4	x 6	x 3	x 8

0	7	3	2	12	5	10	1
x 9	x 9	x 9	x 9	x 9	x 9	x 9	x 9

9	11	8	6	1	4	7	3
x 9	x 9	x 9	x 9	x 9	x 9	x 9	x 9

9 x 9 =   7 x 9 =   4 x 9 =   3 x 9 =   6 x 9 =

5 x 9 =   8 x 9 =   0 x 9 =   1 x 9 =   2 x 9 =

9 x 9 =   9 x 3 =   9 x 8 =   9 x 6 =   9 x 0 =

9 x 4 =   9 x 7 =   9 x 5 =   9 x 2 =   9 x 1 =

1 x 9 =   0 x 9 =   11 x 9 =   12 x 9 =   10 x 9 =

Name _____

Beat the Clock

How quickly can you complete this page? Time yourself. Ready, set, go!

Time : _____
Number Correct : _____

10	10	10	10	10	10	10	10
x 3	x 5	x 9	x 5	x 0	x 7	x 11	x 9

10	10	10	10	10	10	10	10
x 2	x 8	x 10	x 1	x 6	x 4	x 12	x 2

11	7	3	2	5	10	12	7
x 10	x 10	x 10	x 10	x 10	x 10	x 10	x 10

9	0	8	6	1	4	5	9
x 10	x 10	x 10	x 10	x 10	x 10	x 10	x 10

8 x 10 =   0 x 10 =   4 x 10 =   3 x 10 =   6 x 10 =

5 x 10 =   1 x 10 =   7 x 10 =   9 x 10 =   2 x 10 =

10 x 9 =   10 x 3 =   10 x 8 =   10 x 6 =   10 x 0 =

10 x 4 =   10 x 1 =   10 x 5 =   10 x 2 =   10 x 7 =

10 x 6 =   10 x 0 =   10 x 10 =   10 x 11 =   10 x 12 =

Name _____

Beat the Clock

How quickly can you complete this page? Time yourself. Ready, set, go!

Time : _____
Number Correct : _____

11	11	11	11	11	11	11	11
x 3	x 5	x 9	x 10	x 12	x 0	x 6	x 9

11	11	11	11	11	11	11	11
x 2	x 8	x 4	x 1	x 7	x 6	x 11	x 2

6	0	3	2	7	5	12	6
x 11	x 11	x 11	x 11	x 11	x 11	x 11	x 11

9	11	8	6	1	4	10	3
x 11	x 11	x 11	x 11	x 11	x 11	x 11	x 11

9 x 11 =   7 x 11 =   4 x 11 =   3 x 11 =   6 x 11 =

5 x 11 =   8 x 11 =   7 x 11 =   9 x 11 =   2 x 11 =

11 x 2 =   11 x 3 =   11 x 8 =   11 x 6 =   11 x 0 =

11 x 4 =   11 x 1 =   11 x 5 =   11 x 2 =   11 x 1 =

11 x 6 =   11 x 0 =   11 x 10 =   11 x 12 =   11 x 11 =

Name _____

Beat the Clock

How quickly can you complete this page? Time yourself. Ready, set, go!

Time : _____
Number Correct : _____

12	12	12	12	12	12	12	12
x 3	x 11	x 0	x 5	x 10	x 7	x 6	x 9

12	12	12	12	12	12	12	12
x 2	x 8	x 4	x 1	x 12	x 8	x 3	x 7

0	10	3	2	11	7	5	6
x 12	x 12	x 12	x 12	x 12	x 12	x 12	x 12

9	8	12	6	1	4	8	3
x 12	x 12	x 12	x 12	x 12	x 12	x 12	x 12

1 x 12 =   0 x 12 =   4 x 12 =   3 x 12 =   6 x 12 =

5 x 12 =   8 x 12 =   7 x 12 =   9 x 12 =   2 x 12 =

12 x 9 =   12 x 3 =   12 x 8 =   12 x 6 =   12 x 0 =

12 x 4 =   12 x 7 =   12 x 5 =   12 x 2 =   12 x 1 =

12 x 6 =   12 x 0 =   12 x 10 =   12 x 12 =   12 x 11 =

32   CD-3723

Name _____

Multiplication Mania

How quickly can you complete this page? Time yourself. Ready, set, go!

Time : _____
Number Correct : _____

9	4	3	9	6	3	5	2
x 3	x 7	x 8	x 9	x 6	x 6	x 6	x 8

5	7	5	8	2	5	9	7
x 8	x 2	x 5	x 6	x 9	x 3	x 0	x 6

9	8	5	7	9	5	4	1
x 7	x 9	x 4	x 8	x 4	x 7	x 6	x 8

6	7	9	3	8	2	5	1
x 2	x 7	x 6	x 7	x 8	x 8	x 9	x 7

$9 \times 3 =$ $7 \times 5 =$ $4 \times 9 =$ $3 \times 6 =$ $6 \times 7 =$

$5 \times 5 =$ $8 \times 2 =$ $7 \times 4 =$ $9 \times 7 =$ $8 \times 4 =$

$9 \times 2 =$ $3 \times 8 =$ $8 \times 8 =$ $6 \times 6 =$ $6 \times 9 =$

$8 \times 4 =$ $8 \times 9 =$ $8 \times 5 =$ $2 \times 8 =$ $9 \times 5 =$

$1 \times 6 =$ $0 \times 0 =$ $4 \times 6 =$ $7 \times 2 =$ $4 \times 3 =$

33   CD-3723

Multiplication Mania

How quickly can you complete this page? Time yourself. Ready, set, go!

Time : _____
Number Correct : _____

2 x 3	4 x 8	3 x 5	9 x 0	3 x 6	8 x 8	4 x 6	7 x 8
5 x 10	7 x 7	9 x 5	1 x 6	2 x 4	5 x 8	9 x 3	6 x 6
3 x 2	7 x 9	5 x 0	3 x 6	8 x 4	12 x 7	4 x 11	6 x 8
6 x 5	9 x 7	8 x 6	3 x 2	4 x 8	2 x 10	2 x 9	1 x 6

9 x 4 =   8 x 5 =   0 x 9 =   8 x 6 =   11 x 7 =

5 x 7 =   4 x 2 =   7 x 3 =   6 x 7 =   12 x 4 =

5 x 2 =   3 x 3 =   8 x 8 =   3 x 6 =   10 x 9 =

8 x 4 =   4 x 9 =   9 x 5 =   3 x 8 =   11 x 5 =

8 x 6 =   0 x 5 =   4 x 9 =   7 x 7 =   12 x 3 =

Multiplication Mania

How quickly can you complete this page? Time yourself. Ready, set, go!

Time : _____
Number Correct : _____

12	4	3	9	5	10	8	2
x 3	x 8	x 11	x 0	x 7	x 2	x 1	x 8

5	7	12	8	4	7	12	7
x 10	x 9	x 6	x 8	x 9	x 11	x 10	x 6

6	8	6	4	9	5	4	1
x 7	x 5	x 4	x 3	x 7	x 3	x 6	x 8

8	7	11	3	8	2	5	1
x 2	x 4	x 6	x 10	x 4	x 9	x 7	x 7

9 x 4 =	7 x 8 =	7 x 9 =	3 x 3 =	6 x 6 =
5 x 6 =	4 x 2 =	5 x 4 =	4 x 7 =	8 x 8 =
9 x 9 =	3 x 11 =	8 x 6 =	6 x 10 =	3 x 9 =
4 x 4 =	6 x 3 =	9 x 5 =	2 x 8 =	8 x 5 =
5 x 6 =	0 x 10 =	4 x 6 =	7 x 7 =	4 x 3 =

         CD-3723

Multiplication Mania

How quickly can you complete this page? Time yourself. Ready, set, go!

Time : _____
Number Correct : _____

1 x 3	4 x 4	3 x 8	9 x 0	8 x 6	3 x 4	5 x 7	2 x 8
8 x 8	7 x 6	5 x 5	10 x 6	11 x 9	12 x 3	11 x 0	7 x 6
3 x 7	8 x 10	9 x 4	7 x 7	9 x 2	5 x 8	4 x 6	1 x 8
7 x 2	4 x 7	6 x 6	3 x 3	8 x 9	2 x 6	11 x 9	1 x 7

11 x 3 =   7 x 9 =   6 x 9 =   5 x 6 =   2 x 7 =

10 x 5 =   8 x 2 =   7 x 3 =   9 x 5 =   8 x 3 =

9 x 12 =   5 x 8 =   8 x 6 =   4 x 6 =   2 x 9 =

8 x 11 =   8 x 9 =   6 x 7 =   2 x 4 =   3 x 5 =

10 x 3 =   9 x 6 =   3 x 6 =   5 x 4 =   2 x 3 =

Name _____

Skill: Multiplication Facts

Compare Squares

Compare the number sentences. Write <, >, or = in the square to make a true math statement. The first problem is done for you.

1. 2 x 8 [<] 3 x 7   **11.** 6 x 3 [ ] 9 x 2

2. 3 x 4 [ ] 2 x 7   **12.** 2 x 7 [ ] 5 x 3

3. 4 x 5 [ ] 8 x 2   **13.** 5 x 6 [ ] 8 x 4

4. 3 x 9 [ ] 4 x 7   **14.** 7 x 4 [ ] 3 x 8

5. 11 x 2 [ ] 5 x 5   **15.** 8 x 5 [ ] 4 x 11

6. 3 x 3 [ ] 2 x 4   **16.** 6 x 8 [ ] 5 x 9

7. 3 x 8 [ ] 6 x 4   **17.** 3 x 9 [ ] 6 x 4

8. 8 x 2 [ ] 3 x 5   **18.** 8 x 7 [ ] 9 x 6

9. 2 x 12 [ ] 3 x 8   **19.** 4 x 8 [ ] 6 x 6

10. 5 x 3 [ ] 4 x 4   **20.** 10 x 5 [ ] 7 x 7

Compare Squares

Compare the number sentences. Write <, >, or = in the square to make a true math statement. The first problem is done for you.

1. 5 x 4 $<$ 7 x 3   **11.** 6 x 5 ☐ 4 x 7

2. 5 x 7 ☐ 9 x 4   **12.** 4 x 8 ☐ 7 x 5

3. 6 x 5 ☐ 8 x 4   **13.** 4 x 4 ☐ 2 x 8

4. 4 x 3 ☐ 6 x 2   **14.** 7 x 5 ☐ 6 x 6

5. 7 x 4 ☐ 9 x 3   **15.** 6 x 7 ☐ 8 x 3

6. 5 x 8 ☐ 4 x 10   **16.** 4 x 7 ☐ 8 x 5

7. 6 x 7 ☐ 5 x 5   **17.** 9 x 6 ☐ 7 x 8

8. 4 x 8 ☐ 7 x 5   **18.** 4 x 9 ☐ 6 x 6

9. 6 x 6 ☐ 5 x 8   **19.** 5 x 5 ☐ 7 x 3

10. 11 x 5 ☐ 7 x 9   **20.** 8 x 6 ☐ 5 x 9

Compare Squares

Compare the number sentences. Write <, >, or = in the square to make a true math statement. The first problem is done for you.

1.   6 x 6 $\boxed{<}$ 8 x 5

11. 10 x 5 $\square$ 7 x 8

2. 9 x 12 $\square$ 10 x 11

12. 5 x 12 $\square$ 10 x 6

3. 7 x 7 $\square$ 5 x 11

13. 8 x 4 $\square$ 9 x 3

4. 12 x 4 $\square$ 8 x 6

14. 6 x 7 $\square$ 8 x 5

5. 7 x 9 $\square$ 6 x 11

15. 4 x 8 $\square$ 6 x 6

6. 5 x 9 $\square$ 6 x 7

16. 10 x 7 $\square$ 11 x 6

7. 7 x 5 $\square$ 9 x 4

17. 5 x 9 $\square$ 8 x 6

8. 9 x 6 $\square$ 8 x 8

18. 7 x 4 $\square$ 3 x 6

9. 8 x 9 $\square$ 6 x 12

19. 5 x 3 $\square$ 4 x 4

10. 6 x 5 $\square$ 10 x 3

20. 10 x 4 $\square$ 6 x 7

     CD-3723

Compare Squares

Compare the number sentences. Write <, >, or = in the square to make a true math statement. The first problem is done for you.

1. 9 x 4 $\boxed{<}$ 7 x 6

2. 10 x 12 $\square$ 11 x 12

3. 9 x 5 $\square$ 6 x 8

4. 9 x 8 $\square$ 6 x 12

5. 8 x 8 $\square$ 7 x 9

6. 6 x 9 $\square$ 5 x 11

7. 12 x 5 $\square$ 6 x 10

8. 8 x 10 $\square$ 9 x 9

9. 4 x 9 $\square$ 3 x 12

10. 10 x 9 $\square$ 12 x 12

11. 8 x 7 $\square$ 10 x 5

12. 12 x 9 $\square$ 11 x 10

13. 11 x 5 $\square$ 8 x 6

14. 9 x 7 $\square$ 8 x 8

15. 7 x 10 $\square$ 8 x 9

16. 4 x 11 $\square$ 3 x 12

17. 6 x 10 $\square$ 8 x 9

18. 8 x 5 $\square$ 4 x 10

19. 5 x 7 $\square$ 3 x 11

20. 6 x 7 $\square$ 4 x 12

MISSING FACTORS

Solve the problems by filling in the box with a number that will make the math statement true.

1. ☐ x 4 = 16   11. ☐ x 9 = 36   21. ☐ x 4 = 8

2. ☐ x 10 = 20   12. ☐ x 7 = 21   22. ☐ x 3 = 15

3. ☐ x 3 = 24   13. ☐ x 6 = 30   23. ☐ x 3 = 9

4. ☐ x 6 = 36   14. ☐ x 12 = 24   24. ☐ x 6 = 42

5. ☐ x 5 = 35   15. ☐ x 11 = 33   25. ☐ x 7 = 49

6. ☐ x 8 = 32   16. ☐ x 8 = 16   26. ☐ x 3 = 18

7. ☐ x 2 = 18   17. ☐ x 6 = 24   27. ☐ x 8 = 24

8. ☐ x 2 = 22   18. ☐ x 5 = 25   28. ☐ x 4 = 20

9. ☐ x 7 = 28   19. ☐ x 3 = 27   29. ☐ x 7 = 35

10. ☐ x 4 = 20   20. ☐ x 6 = 12   30. ☐ x 9 = 36

MISSING FACTORS

Solve the problems by filling in the box with a number that will make the
math statement true.

1. ☐ x 7 = 21   **11.** ☐ x 7 = 35   **21.** ☐ x 6 = 54

2. ☐ x 9 = 45   **12.** ☐ x 6 = 36   **22.** ☐ x 10 = 70

3. ☐ x 12 = 36   **13.** ☐ x 12 = 48   **23.** ☐ x 4 = 12

4. ☐ x 4 = 32   **14.** ☐ x 6 = 60   **24.** ☐ x 6 = 42

5. ☐ x 3 = 15   **15.** ☐ x 7 = 84   **25.** ☐ x 8 = 40

6. ☐ x 8 = 32   **16.** ☐ x 12 = 72   **26.** ☐ x 11 = 55

7. ☐ x 7 = 63   **17.** ☐ x 7 = 28   **27.** ☐ x 7 = 56

8. ☐ x 5 = 50   **18.** ☐ x 6 = 48   **28.** ☐ x 4 = 40

9. ☐ x 7 = 56   **19.** ☐ x 5 = 60   **29.** ☐ x 9 = 81

10. ☐ x 9 = 54   **20.** ☐ x 6 = 24   **30.** ☐ x 11 = 22

MISSING FACTORS

Solve the problems by filling in the box with a number that will make the
math statement true.

1. ☐ x 3 = 36   11. ☐ x 3 = 18   21. ☐ x 12 = 60

2. ☐ x 9 = 81   12. ☐ x 8 = 72   22. ☐ x 4 = 32

3. ☐ x 9 = 72   13. ☐ x 4 = 36   23. ☐ x 4 = 40

4. ☐ x 7 = 56   14. ☐ x 4 = 24   24. ☐ x 8 = 32

5. ☐ x 8 = 64   15. ☐ x 4 = 20   25. ☐ x 7 = 63

6. ☐ x 4 = 28   16. ☐ x 5 = 35   26. ☐ x 5 = 45

7. ☐ x 10 = 20   17. ☐ x 10 = 60   27. ☐ x 11 = 88

8. ☐ x 9 = 63   18. ☐ x 6 = 36   28. ☐ x 6 = 12

9. ☐ x 5 = 40   19. ☐ x 2 = 18   29. ☐ x 2 = 24

10. ☐ x 6 = 72   20. ☐ x 2 = 24   30. ☐ x 9 = 18

MISSING FACTORS

Solve the problems by filling in the box with a number that will make the
math statement true.

1. ☐ x 7 = 56   **11.** ☐ x 6 = 36   **21.** ☐ x 12 = 144

2. ☐ x 12 = 48   **12.** ☐ x 7 = 35   **22.** ☐ x 11 = 88

3. ☐ x 9 = 45   **13.** ☐ x 5 = 45   **23.** ☐ x 12 = 108

4. ☐ x 5 = 60   **14.** ☐ x 8 = 72   **24.** ☐ x 10 = 100

5. ☐ x 9 = 81   **15.** ☐ x 7 = 84   **25.** ☐ x 12 = 120

6. ☐ x 8 = 64   **16.** ☐ x 6 = 54   **26.** ☐ x 11 = 121

7. ☐ x 4 = 16   **17.** ☐ x 8 = 96   **27.** ☐ x 11 = 132

8. ☐ x 5 = 40   **18.** ☐ x 7 = 49   **28.** ☐ x 10 = 120

9. ☐ x 3 = 27   **19.** ☐ x 6 = 72   **29.** ☐ x 12 = 96

10. ☐ x 2 = 24   **20.** ☐ x 4 = 32   **30.** ☐ x 10 = 110

Mystery Math

Look at the mystery number. Circle all math expressions in that row which equal the mystery number. The first problem is done for you.

Mystery Number	Math Expression			
6	3 x 3	(6 x 1)	2 x 2	(3 x 2)
18	4 x 7	2 x 9	3 x 6	8 x 2
20	5 x 5	10 x 2	4 x 4	5 x 4
36	3 x 12	6 x 5	4 x 9	6 x 6
45	7 x 5	5 x 8	12 x 4	9 x 5
21	8 x 2	3 x 7	9 x 3	4 x 4
12	6 x 3	3 x 3	2 x 6	4 x 5
24	6 x 6	8 x 3	5 x 5	2 x 12
48	6 x 7	9 x 6	8 x 6	4 x 12

Mystery Math

Look at the mystery number. Circle all math expressions in that row which equal the mystery number. The first problem is done for you.

Mystery Number	Math Expression			
8	3 x 3	(2 x 4)	6 x 2	(1 x 8)
25	8 x 3	6 x 4	5 x 5	2 x 11
12	6 x 2	3 x 3	4 x 3	1 x 12
42	12 x 4	6 x 7	8 x 6	7 x 6
60	5 x 12	12 x 6	8 x 8	10 x 6
27	3 x 9	4 x 7	3 x 8	7 x 3
32	12 x 4	8 x 4	11 x 3	6 x 5
56	12 x 4	6 x 9	7 x 8	9 x 5
54	12 x 4	6 x 9	7 x 8	9 x 5

Mystery Math

Look at the mystery number. Circle all math expressions in that row which equal the mystery number. The first problem is done for you.

Mystery Number	Math Expression			
48	6 x 6	(12 x 4)	7 x 5	(6 x 8)
108	9 x 10	11 x 12	12 x 9	11 x 11
81	7 x 11	7 x 6	8 x 9	9 x 9
56	5 x 6	12 x 4	6 x 9	8 x 7
100	9 x 9	5 x 12	10 x 10	11 x 10
72	12 x 6	9 x 8	8 x 8	7 x 9
40	6 x 7	8 x 5	10 x 4	12 x 4
54	8 x 7	5 x 4	6 x 9	8 x 6
84	8 x 4	11 x 8	7 x 9	7 x 12

Mystery Math

Look at the mystery number. Circle all math expressions in that row which equal the mystery number. The first problem is done for you.

Mystery Number	Math Expression			
144	12 x 11	(12 x 12)	11 x 11	4 x 4
120	11 x 11	11 x 12	10 x 11	12 x 10
60	6 x 10	12 x 6	6 x 11	12 x 5
121	12 x 11	11 x 10	11 x 11	10 x 12
56	6 x 9	8 x 8	9 x 7	7 x 8
132	12 x 12	12 x 13	11 x 12	11 x 11
110	11 x 11	11 x 10	11 x 12	11 x 11
72	12 x 7	12 x 6	8 x 9	9 x 9
96	11 x 6	12 x 9	9 x 11	8 x 12

Name _____

Leapfrog

Use your math facts to move across the lily pads.

1. 7 x 1 = $\bigcirc$ x 4 = $\bigcirc$

2. 2 x 2 = $\bigcirc$ x 4 = $\bigcirc$

3. 3 x 3 = $\bigcirc$ x 2 = $\bigcirc$

4. 4 x 2 = $\bigcirc$ x 4 = $\bigcirc$

5. 1 x 5 = $\bigcirc$ x 11 = $\bigcirc$

6. 2 x 3 = $\bigcirc$ x 2 = $\bigcirc$

7. 2 x 2 = $\bigcirc$ x 6 = $\bigcirc$

8. 4 x 2 = $\bigcirc$ x 3 = $\bigcirc$

9. 6 x 2 = $\bigcirc$ x 2 = $\bigcirc$

10. 2 x 2 = $\bigcirc$ x 3 = $\bigcirc$

Bonus

$$\begin{array}{r} 3 \\ \times\ 2 \\ \hline \square \end{array}$$

$$\begin{array}{r} \times\ 2 \\ \hline \square \end{array}$$

$$\begin{array}{r} \times\ 3 \\ \hline \square \end{array}$$

CD-3723

Leapfrog

Use your math facts to move across the lily pads.

1. 4 x 3 = ⬭ x 5 = ⬭

2. 2 x 4 = ⬭ x 8 = ⬭

3. 3 x 2 = ⬭ x 4 = ⬭

4. 2 x 2 = ⬭ x 3 = ⬭

5. 4 x 2 = ⬭ x 4 = ⬭

6. 1 x 3 = ⬭ x 6 = ⬭

7. 4 x 0 = ⬭ x 5 = ⬭

8. 3 x 2 = ⬭ x 7 = ⬭

9. 5 x 2 = ⬭ x 6 = ⬭

10. 3 x 4 = ⬭ x 7 = ⬭

Bonus

$$
\begin{array}{r}
1 \\
\times\ 5 \\
\hline
\end{array}
$$

$$
\begin{array}{r}
\times\ 2 \\
\hline
\end{array}
$$

$$
\begin{array}{r}
\times\ 6 \\
\hline
\end{array}
$$

Name _____

Leapfrog

Use your math facts to move across the lily pads.

1. 2 x 2 = ⬭ x 2 = ⬭

2. 3 x 2 = ⬭ x 7 = ⬭

3. 2 x 5 = ⬭ x 9 = ⬭

4. 3 x 3 = ⬭ x 6 = ⬭

5. 3 x 2 = ⬭ x 4 = ⬭

6. 4 x 3 = ⬭ x 3 = ⬭

7. 2 x 2 = ⬭ x 12 = ⬭

8. 4 x 2 = ⬭ x 8 = ⬭

9. 6 x 2 = ⬭ x 7 = ⬭

10. 3 x 3 = ⬭ x 9 = ⬭

Bonus

$$\begin{array}{r} 3 \\ \times\ 3 \\ \hline \square \end{array}$$

$$\begin{array}{r} \times\ 1 \\ \hline \square \end{array}$$

$$\begin{array}{r} \times\ 6 \\ \hline \square \end{array}$$

CD-3723

Skill: Multiplication Facts

Leapfrog
Use your math facts to move across the lily pads.

1. 2 x 3 = ⬭ x 5 = ⬭

2. 4 x 2 = ⬭ x 6 = ⬭

3. 2 x 5 = ⬭ x 11 = ⬭

4. 2 x 2 = ⬭ x 7 = ⬭

5. 3 x 3 = ⬭ x 12 = ⬭

6. 4 x 3 = ⬭ x 4 = ⬭

7. 2 x 4 = ⬭ x 7 = ⬭

8. 6 x 2 = ⬭ x 12 = ⬭

9. 3 x 3 = ⬭ x 8 = ⬭

10. 2 x 3 = ⬭ x 7 = ⬭

Bonus

$$\begin{array}{r} 2 \\ \times\ 2 \\ \hline \end{array}$$

$$\begin{array}{r} \times\ 2 \\ \hline \end{array}$$

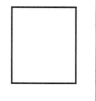

$$\begin{array}{r} \times\ 9 \\ \hline \end{array}$$

CD-3723

Skill: Multiplication Facts

Leapfrog

Use your math facts to move across the lily pads.

1. 5 x 1 = $\bigcirc$ x 8 = $\bigcirc$

2. 3 x 3 = $\bigcirc$ x 6 = $\bigcirc$

3. 2 x 3 = $\bigcirc$ x 11 = $\bigcirc$

4. 4 x 3 = $\bigcirc$ x 9 = $\bigcirc$

5. 2 x 4 = $\bigcirc$ x 7 = $\bigcirc$

6. 2 x 2 = $\bigcirc$ x 8 = $\bigcirc$

7. 5 x 2 = $\bigcirc$ x 3 = $\bigcirc$

8. 3 x 2 = $\bigcirc$ x 5 = $\bigcirc$

9. 5 x 2 = $\bigcirc$ x 10 = $\bigcirc$

10. 7 x 1 = $\bigcirc$ x 7 = $\bigcirc$

Bonus

$$\begin{array}{r} 6 \\ \times\ 1 \\ \hline \square \end{array}$$

$$\begin{array}{r} \times\ 2 \\ \hline \square \end{array}$$

$$\begin{array}{r} \times\ 5 \\ \hline \square \end{array}$$

Leapfrog

Use your math facts to move across the lily pads.

1. 4 x 1 = ⬭ x 5 = ⬭

2. 3 x 3 = ⬭ x 7 = ⬭

3. 2 x 3 = ⬭ x 6 = ⬭

4. 4 x 3 = ⬭ x 8 = ⬭

5. 2 x 5 = ⬭ x 10 = ⬭

6. 2 x 2 = ⬭ x 9 = ⬭

7. 3 x 3 = ⬭ x 9 = ⬭

8. 6 x 2 = ⬭ x 11 = ⬭

9. 4 x 2 = ⬭ x 7 = ⬭

10. 3 x 2 = ⬭ x 8 = ⬭

Bonus

5
x
1
_____
▢

x
2
_____
▢

x
8
_____
▢

Hopscotch

Use your math facts to complete the hopscotch board.

1. 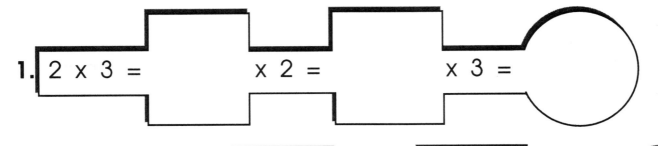 2 x 3 =   x 2 =   x 3 =

2. 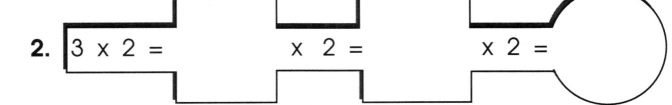 3 x 2 =   x 2 =   x 2 =

3. 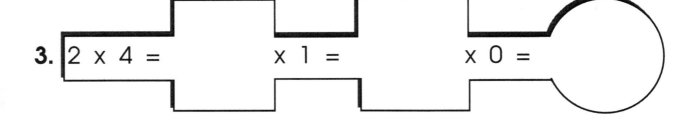 2 x 4 =   x 1 =   x 0 =

4. 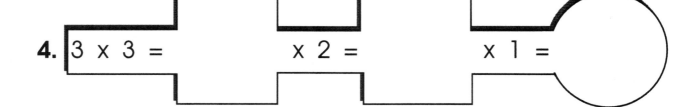 3 x 3 =   x 2 =   x 1 =

5. 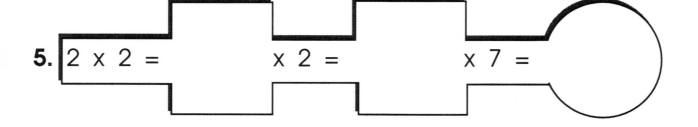 2 x 2 =   x 2 =   x 7 =

6. 2 x 3 =   x 2 =   x 4 =

Hopscotch

Use your math facts to complete the hopscotch board.

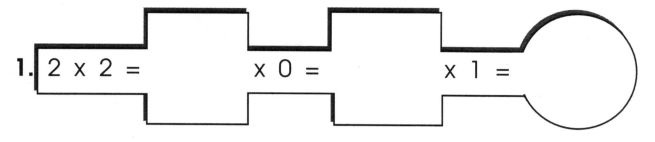

1. 2 x 2 =   x 0 =   x 1 =

2. 1 x 1 =   x 3 =   x 4 =

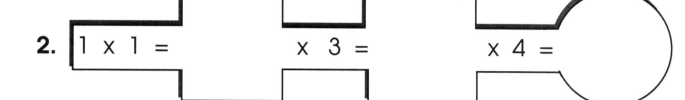

3. 4 x 1 =   x 1 =   x 3 =

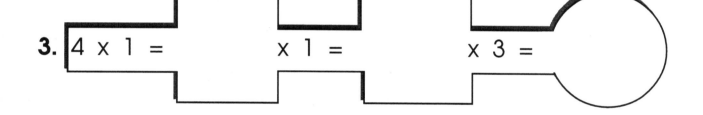

4. 3 x 1 =   x 1 =   x 2 =

5. 2 x 2 =   x 3 =   x 2 =

6. 0 x 0 =   x 2 =   x 3 =

CD-3723

Hopscotch

Use your math facts to complete the hopscotch board.

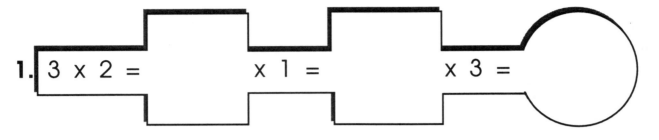

1. 3 x 2 =   x 1 =   x 3 =

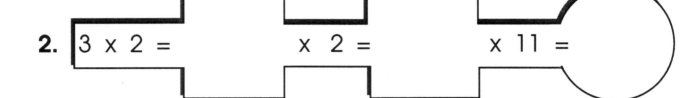

2. 3 x 2 =   x 2 =   x 11 =

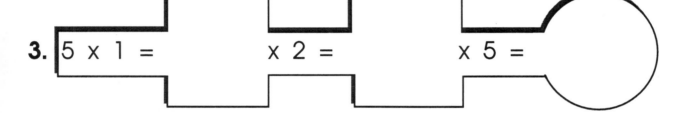

3. 5 x 1 =   x 2 =   x 5 =

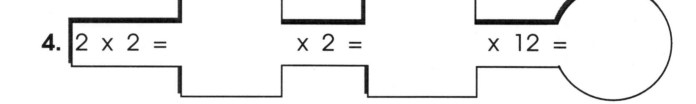

4. 2 x 2 =   x 2 =   x 12 =

5. 2 x 2 =   x 2 =   x 4 =

6. 3 x 3 =   x 1 =   x 7 =

CD-3723

Skill: Multiplication Facts

Hopscotch

Use your math facts to complete the hopscotch board.

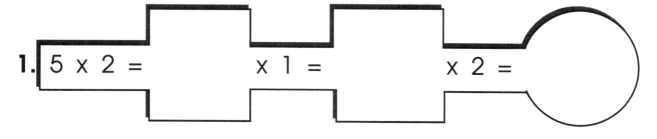

1. 5 x 2 =   x 1 =   x 2 =

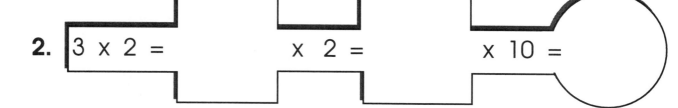

2. 3 x 2 =   x 2 =   x 10 =

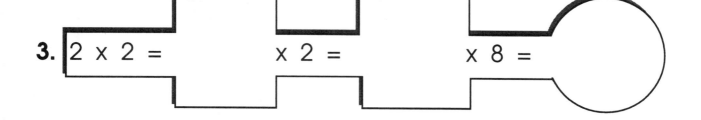

3. 2 x 2 =   x 2 =   x 8 =

4. 2 x 2 =   x 3 =   x 7 =

5. 5 x 1 =   x 2 =   x 6 =

6. 2 x 2 =   x 3 =   x 11 =

CD-3723

Name _____

Blankety- Blanks

Solve the problems below and write the answer in the box. On the blanket,
shade in all the numbers that are in the answer boxes.
The answers will make a pattern.

6 x 5 = ☐

4 x 7 = ☐

3 x 6 = ☐

5 x 12 = ☐

3 x 9 = ☐

4 x 6 = ☐

9 x 5 = ☐

3 x 11 = ☐

5 x 5 = ☐

4 x 4 = ☐

3 x 7 = ☐

8 x 5 = ☐

4 x 8 = ☐

7 x 5 = ☐

3 x 5 = ☐

4 x 9 = ☐

11	50	44	31
30	4	59	25
33	19	47	16
45	13	34	21
28	10	83	40
18	29	14	32
24	37	55	35
27	41	37	15
60	19	61	36
19	23	8	9

Blankety- Blanks

Solve the problems below and write the answer in the box. On the blanket, shade in all the numbers that are in the answer boxes.
The answers will make a pattern.

$4 \times 3 =$ ☐

$6 \times 9 =$ ☐

$7 \times 8 =$ ☐

$5 \times 12 =$ ☐

$6 \times 8 =$ ☐

$7 \times 12 =$ ☐

$7 \times 7 =$ ☐

$6 \times 12 =$ ☐

$7 \times 9 =$ ☐

$6 \times 6 =$ ☐

$6 \times 7 =$ ☐

$9 \times 5 =$ ☐

$7 \times 3 =$ ☐

$6 \times 11 =$ ☐

$4 \times 7 =$ ☐

$6 \times 5 =$ ☐

48	20	33	60
15	12	84	88
29	36	56	16
41	53	74	17
29	42	66	40
38	28	45	43
14	92	85	61
46	63	21	10
62	54	30	70
72	33	18	49

CD-3723

Blankety- Blanks

Solve the problems below and write the answer in the box. On the blanket, shade in all the numbers that are in the answer boxes.
The answers will make a pattern.

6 x 3 = ☐

9 x 12 = ☐

8 x 8 = ☐

10 x 12 = ☐

7 x 12 = ☐

10 x 6 = ☐

9 x 9 = ☐

10 x 11 = ☐

9 x 8 = ☐

7 x 9 = ☐

7 x 7 = ☐

8 x 12 = ☐

5 x 9 = ☐

9 x 6 = ☐

10 x 10 = ☐

7 x 8 = ☐

11	56	52	100
18	43	108	25
39	120	47	49
64	51	63	26
28	60	82	45
84	58	96	101
22	110	55	100
81	31	54	75
65	72	101	56
99	83	29	79

Blankety- Blanks

Solve the problems below and write the answer in the box. On the blanket, shade in all the numbers that are in the answer boxes.
The answers will make a pattern.

8 x 4 = ☐

6 x 12 = ☐

8 x 6 = ☐

10 x 12 = ☐

11 x 12 = ☐

7 x 6 = ☐

9 x 12 = ☐

11 x 11 = ☐

8 x 5 = ☐

4 x 9 = ☐

8 x 12 = ☐

7 x 9 = ☐

12 x 12 = ☐

9 x 9 = ☐

7 x 12 = ☐

10 x 10 = ☐

120	32	84	72
20	74	59	23
81	48	144	100
43	11	37	57
63	132	96	42
17	39	73	69
36	108	40	121
22	102	77	35
61	29	66	46
38	26	78	29

CD-3723

Renaming Multiplication Practice

Complete the problems below. Remember to rename numbers when needed.

15	26	18	12	27	22	32	41
x 5	x 3	x 4	x 9	x 2	x 5	x 4	x 5

23	19	37	16	71	54	33	28
x 3	x 5	x 3	x 7	x 6	x 2	x 4	x 3

43	51	36	84	21	33	56	62
x 9	x 7	x 8	x 4	x 6	x 7	x 3	x 4

39	28	52	67	41	34	18	23
x 2	x 6	x 4	x 5	x 8	x 9	x 5	x 6

6 x 12 =   5 x 42 =   4 x 75 =   3 x 38 =   7 x 44 =

5 x 83 =   8 x 32 =   7 x 56 =   9 x 18 =   2 x 57 =

22 x 9 =   54 x 3 =   73 x 8 =   94 x 6 =   45 x 3 =

74 x 4 =   58 x 7 =   43 x 5 =   98 x 2 =   77 x 4 =

56 x 6 =   97 x 3 =   84 x 6 =   27 x 5 =   51 x 9 =

Name _____

Renaming Multiplication Practice

Complete the problems below. Remember to rename numbers when needed.

42	46	37	32	54	67	84	73
x 5	x 6	x 7	x 8	x 2	x 3	x 4	x 5

37	52	75	49	63	51	44	29
x 4	x 3	x 2	x 5	x 7	x 8	x 7	x 4

123	315	182	143	224	615	428	423
x 4	x 2	x 5	x 3	x 4	x 6	x 3	x 2

129	217	318	456	185	277	189	323
x 4	x 3	x 7	x 5	x 8	x 4	x 5	x 6

6 x 123 =   5 x 242 =   4 x 375 =   3 x 538 =

5 x 383 =   8 x 132 =   7 x 456 =   9 x 182 =

222 x 9 =   544 x 3 =   732 x 8 =   294 x 6 =

574 x 4 =   258 x 7 =   643 x 5 =   798 x 2 =

256 x 6 =   197 x 3 =   484 x 6 =   627 x 5 =

Skill: Multiplication/Division

Leapfrog

Use your math facts to move across the lily pads.

1. $14 \div 2 =$ ⬭ x 3 = ⬭

2. $3 \times 12 =$ ⬭ $\div 6 =$ ⬭

3. $24 \div 6 =$ ⬭ x 8 = ⬭

4. $30 \div 5 =$ ⬭ x 3 = ⬭

5. $5 \times 8 =$ ⬭ $\div 4 =$ ⬭

6. $18 \div 3 =$ ⬭ x 6 = ⬭

7. $2 \times 6 =$ ⬭ $\div 3 =$ ⬭

8. $16 \div 4 =$ ⬭ x 9 = ⬭

9. $28 \div 4 =$ ⬭ x 5 = ⬭

10. $8 \times 3 =$ ⬭ $\div 2 =$ ⬭

Bonus

25

$\div$

5

x

4

$\div$

2

CD-3723

Leapfrog

Use your math facts to move across the lily pads.

1. 40 ÷ 4 = ⬭ x 5 = ⬭

2. 64 ÷ 8 = ⬭ x 7 = ⬭

3. 5 x 4 = ⬭ ÷ 10 = ⬭

4. 6 x 8 = ⬭ ÷ 4 = ⬭

5. 72 ÷ 8 = ⬭ x 5 = ⬭

6. 24 ÷ 4 = ⬭ x 9 = ⬭

7. 6 x 6 = ⬭ ÷ 4 = ⬭

8. 56 ÷ 7 = ⬭ x 4 = ⬭

9. 5 x 12 = ⬭ ÷ 6 = ⬭

10. 48 ÷ 8 = ⬭ x 6 = ⬭

Bonus

54
÷
6
_____
[ ]

x
4
_____
[ ]

÷
9
_____
[ ]

CD-3723

Skill: Multiplication/Division

Leapfrog

Use your math facts to move across the lily pads.

1. $100 \div 10 =$ ⬭ x 9 = ⬭

2. 9 x 8 = ⬭ $\div 12 =$ ⬭

3. 5 x 12 = ⬭ $\div 10 =$ ⬭

4. $63 \div 9 =$ ⬭ x 7 = ⬭

5. 6 x 6 = ⬭ $\div 9 =$ ⬭

6. $81 \div 9 =$ ⬭ x 12 = ⬭

7. $132 \div 11 =$ ⬭ x 6 = ⬭

8. $84 \div 7 =$ ⬭ x 3 = ⬭

9. $108 \div 12 =$ ⬭ x 3 = ⬭

10. 12 x 4 = ⬭ $\div 6 =$ ⬭

Bonus

$$\begin{array}{r} 5 \\ \times\ 2 \\ \hline \end{array}$$

$$\begin{array}{r} \times\ 4 \\ \hline \end{array}$$

$$\begin{array}{r} \div\ 1 \\ \hline \end{array}$$

Name _____

Leapfrog

Use your math facts to move across the lily pads.

1. $144 \div 12 =$ ⬭ $\times$ 8 $=$ ⬭

2. $6 \times 12 =$ ⬭ $\div$ 9 $=$ ⬭

3. $132 \div 12 =$ ⬭ $\times$ 5 $=$ ⬭

4. $5 \times 8 =$ ⬭ $\div 10 =$ ⬭

5. $81 \div 9 =$ ⬭ $\times$ 8 $=$ ⬭

6. $3 \times 12 =$ ⬭ $\div$ 4 $=$ ⬭

7. $110 \div 11 =$ ⬭ $\times$ 3 $=$ ⬭

8. $44 \div 4 =$ ⬭ $\times 12 =$ ⬭

9. $12 \times 5 =$ ⬭ $\div 10 =$ ⬭

10. $4 \times 12 =$ ⬭ $\div$ 8 $=$ ⬭

Bonus

120

$\div$

10

____

☐

$\div$

4

____

☐

$\times$

9

____

☐

CD-3723

Magic Trail

Follow the trail by solving math problems and find the magic number.

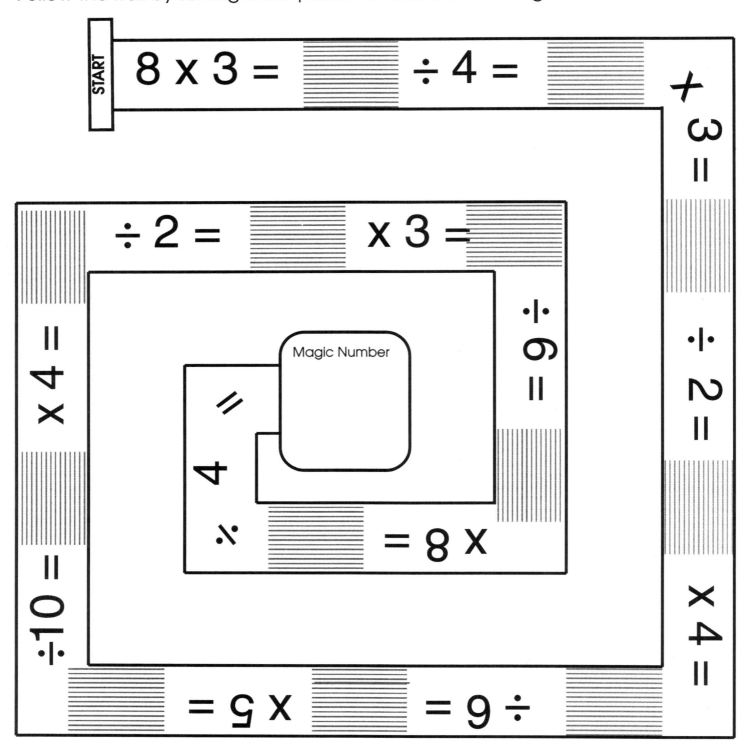

START

$8 \times 3 =$

$\div 4 =$

$\times 3 =$

$\div 2 =$

$\times 3 =$

$\div 6 =$

$\times 4 =$

$\div 2 =$

Magic Number

$=$

4

$\div$

$= 8 \times$

$\div 10 =$

$\times 4 =$

$= 5 \times$

$= 9 \div$

MAGIC NUMBER _____

CD-3723

Magic Trail

Follow the trail by solving math problems and find the magic number.

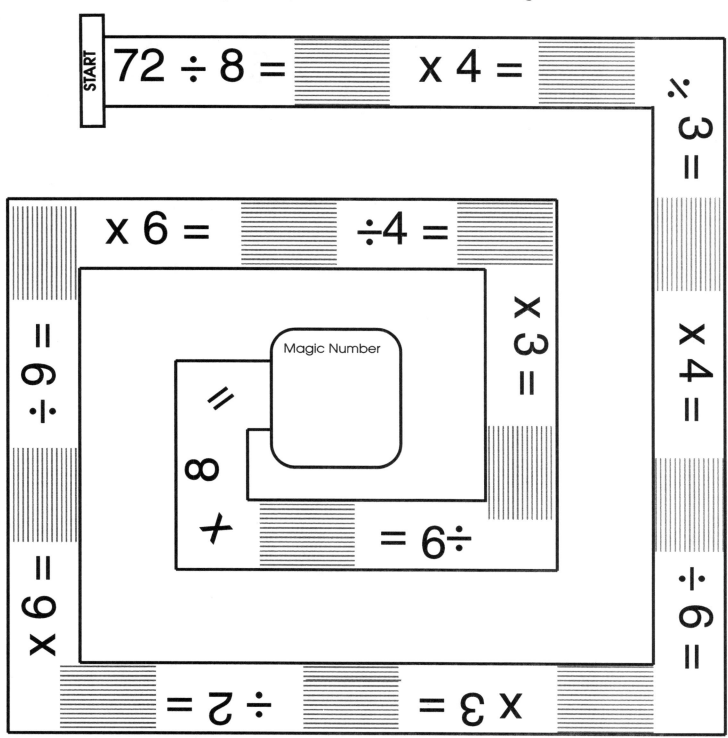

MAGIC NUMBER _____

CD-3723

Magic Trail

Follow the trail by solving math problems and find the magic number.

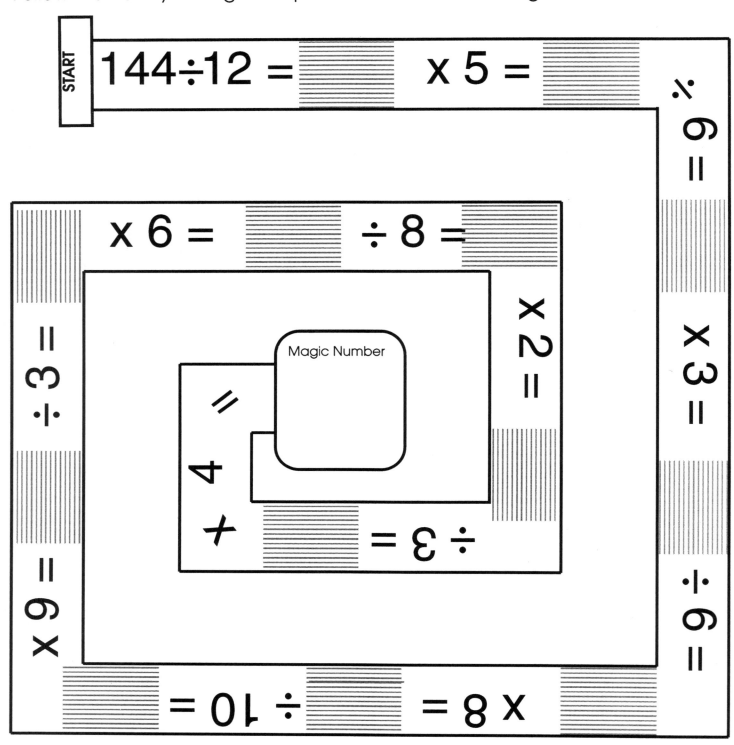

MAGIC NUMBER _____

Family Facts Fiesta

Complete the families of math facts.

□ x 3 = 27
3 x 9 = □
27 ÷ □ = 3
□ ÷ 3 = 9

12 x □ = 24
□ x 2 = 24
24 ÷ 2 = □
□ ÷ 2 = 12

□ x 4 = 24
6 x □ = 24
□ ÷ 4 = 6
24 ÷ □ = 4

□ x 8 = 24
□ x 3 = 24
24 ÷ □ = 8
□ ÷ 8 = 3

7 x □ = 28
□ x 4 = 28
28 ÷ □ = 7
□ ÷ 7 = 4

□ x 3 = 36
□ x 12 = 36
□ ÷ 3 = 12
36 ÷ □ = 3

Bonus:

Can you make two family facts of your own?

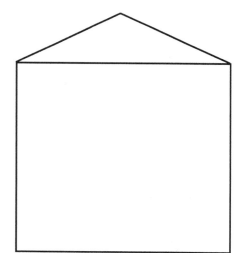

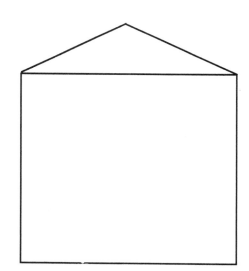

Family Facts Fiesta

Complete the families of math facts.

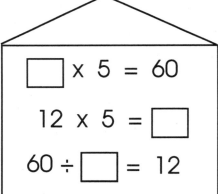

$\square$ x 5 = 60

12 x 5 = $\square$

60 ÷ $\square$ = 12

$\square$ ÷ 12 = 5

6 x $\square$ = 54

$\square$ x 9 = 54

54 ÷ 9 = $\square$

$\square$ ÷ 6 = 9

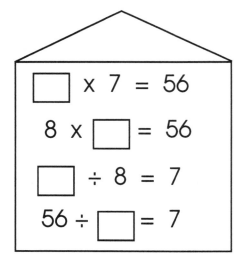

$\square$ x 7 = 56

8 x $\square$ = 56

$\square$ ÷ 8 = 7

56 ÷ $\square$ = 7

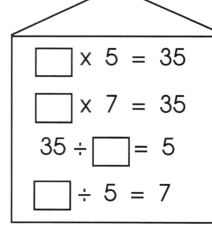

$\square$ x 5 = 35

$\square$ x 7 = 35

35 ÷ $\square$ = 5

$\square$ ÷ 5 = 7

6 x $\square$ = 48

6 x 8 = $\square$

48 ÷ $\square$ = 8

48 ÷ $\square$ = 6

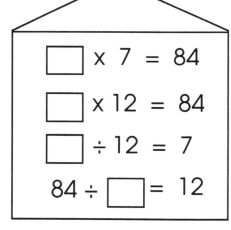

$\square$ x 7 = 84

$\square$ x 12 = 84

$\square$ ÷ 12 = 7

84 ÷ $\square$ = 12

Bonus:

Can you make two family facts of your own?

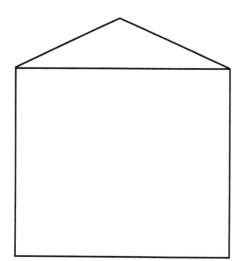

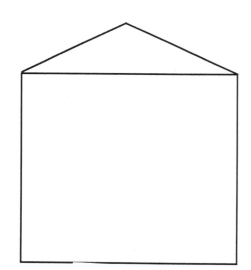

Family Facts Fiesta

Complete the families of math facts.

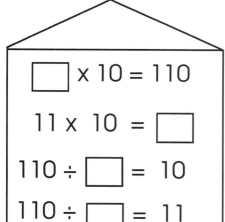

$\square \times 10 = 110$

$11 \times 10 = \square$

$110 \div \square = 10$

$110 \div \square = 11$

$12 \times \square = 108$

$\square \times 9 = 108$

$108 \div 9 = \square$

$\square \div 12 = 9$

$\square \times 12 = 96$

$8 \times \square = 96$

$\square \div 9 = 12$

$96 \div \square = 9$

$\square \times 8 = 72$

$\square \times 9 = 72$

$72 \div \square = 9$

$\square \div 9 = 8$

$12 \times \square = 132$

$12 \times 11 = \square$

$132 \div \square = 11$

$132 \div \square = 12$

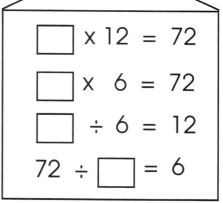

$\square \times 12 = 72$

$\square \times 6 = 72$

$\square \div 6 = 12$

$72 \div \square = 6$

Bonus:

Can you make two family facts of your own?

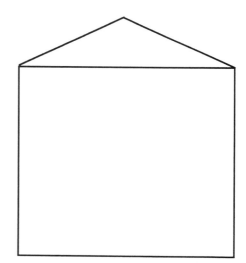

Mystery Math

Look at the mystery number. Circle all math expressions in that row wich equal the mystery number. The first problem is done for you.

Mystery Number	Math Expression			
6	35 ÷ 7	(12 ÷ 2)	(18 ÷ 3)	(2 x 3)
7	64 ÷ 8	56 ÷ 8	27 ÷ 3	32 ÷ 4
5	42 ÷ 6	60 ÷ 12	35 ÷ 5	25 ÷ 5
12	96 ÷ 8	4 x 4	144 ÷ 12	3 x 4
24	4 x 6	3 x 8	120 ÷ 12	10 x 4
9	63 ÷ 7	3 x 3	72 ÷ 9	81 ÷ 9
11	6 x 2	44 ÷ 4	121 ÷ 11	120 ÷ 10
12	72 ÷ 8	60 ÷ 6	3 x 4	48 ÷ 4
10	2 x 6	100 ÷ 10	2 x 5	120 ÷ 10

Mystery Math

Look at the mystery number. Circle all math expressions in that row wich equal the mystery number. The first problem is done for you.

Mystery Number	Math Expression			
3	$12 \div 6$	2×4	$(15 \div 5)$	$(21 \div 7)$
11	4×7	$77 \div 7$	$30 \div 3$	$132 \div 12$
5	$60 \div 12$	4×2	$55 \div 11$	$28 \div 7$
12	6×2	$132 \div 11$	$60 \div 6$	4×4
9	$80 \div 8$	3×3	$81 \div 9$	$72 \div 8$
7	$28 \div 4$	$49 \div 7$	3×2	$27 \div 3$
10	$60 \div 10$	2×5	$45 \div 5$	$110 \div 11$
12	$60 \div 5$	3×4	12×1	$120 \div 10$
8	$24 \div 4$	3×5	$32 \div 4$	8×0

Skill: Multiplication/Division

MISSING FACTORS

Solve the problems by filling in the box with a number that will make the math statement true.

1. ☐ ÷ 6 = 2   11. ☐ ÷ 2 = 12   21. ☐ ÷ 4 = 10

2. ☐ ÷ 3 = 6   12. ☐ ÷ 7 = 5   22. ☐ ÷ 9 = 4

3. ☐ ÷ 5 = 8   13. ☐ ÷ 9 = 3   23. ☐ ÷ 3 = 12

4. ☐ ÷ 4 = 5   14. ☐ ÷ 5 = 2   24. ☐ ÷ 5 = 3

5. ☐ ÷ 6 = 6   15. ☐ ÷ 6 = 8   25. ☐ ÷ 7 = 8

6. ☐ ÷ 9 = 5   16. ☐ ÷ 5 = 5   26. ☐ ÷ 4 = 10

7. ☐ ÷ 7 = 3   17. ☐ ÷ 6 = 6   27. ☐ ÷ 9 = 4

8. ☐ ÷ 3 = 12   18. ☐ ÷ 7 = 4   28. ☐ ÷ 2 = 8

9. ☐ ÷ 6 = 7   19. ☐ ÷ 6 = 9   29. ☐ ÷ 5 = 8

10. ☐ ÷ 8 = 4   20. ☐ ÷ 3 = 8   30. ☐ ÷ 7 = 2

MISSING FACTORS

Solve the problems by filling in the box with a number that will make the
math statement true.

1. ☐ ÷ 7 = 10   11. ☐ ÷ 7 = 3   21. ☐ ÷ 9 = 8

2. ☐ ÷ 6 = 8   12. ☐ ÷ 9 = 12   22. ☐ ÷ 11 = 11

3. ☐ ÷ 12 = 10   13. ☐ ÷ 7 = 8   23. ☐ ÷ 7 = 7

4. ☐ ÷ 6 = 9   14. ☐ ÷ 8 = 5   24. ☐ ÷ 5 = 8

5. ☐ ÷ 8 = 6   15. ☐ ÷ 10 = 11   25. ☐ ÷ 10 = 9

6. ☐ ÷ 8 = 12   16. ☐ ÷ 11 = 7   26. ☐ ÷ 4 = 12

7. ☐ ÷ 9 = 7   17. ☐ ÷ 7 = 6   27. ☐ ÷ 9 = 9

8. ☐ ÷ 4 = 9   18. ☐ ÷ 12 = 9   28. ☐ ÷ 12 = 6

9. ☐ ÷ 8 = 8   19. ☐ ÷ 9 = 9   29. ☐ ÷ 5 = 8

10. ☐ ÷ 10 = 10 20. ☐ ÷ 7 = 12   30. ☐ ÷ 9 = 2

MISSING FACTORS

Solve the problems by filling in the box with a number that will make the math statement true.

1. $\boxed{} \div 4 = 8$

2. $\boxed{} \div 9 = 6$

3. $\boxed{} \div 8 = 8$

4. $\boxed{} \div 11 = 5$

5. $\boxed{} \div 8 = 7$

6. $\boxed{} \div 9 = 8$

7. $\boxed{} \div 10 = 11$

8. $\boxed{} \div 12 = 11$

9. $\boxed{} \div 7 = 12$

10. $\boxed{} \div 11 = 11$

11. $\boxed{} \div 12 = 9$

12. $\boxed{} \div 8 = 11$

13. $\boxed{} \div 8 = 6$

14. $\boxed{} \div 10 = 12$

15. $\boxed{} \div 12 = 4$

16. $\boxed{} \div 11 = 12$

17. $\boxed{} \div 9 = 6$

18. $\boxed{} \div 3 = 9$

19. $\boxed{} \div 9 = 7$

20. $\boxed{} \div 12 = 12$

21. $\boxed{} \div 4 = 11$

22. $\boxed{} \div 9 = 9$

23. $\boxed{} \div 10 = 10$

24. $\boxed{} \div 5 = 3$

25. $\boxed{} \div 9 = 10$

26. $\boxed{} \div 5 = 12$

27. $\boxed{} \div 7 = 11$

28. $\boxed{} \div 10 = 3$

29. $\boxed{} \div 5 = 10$

30. $\boxed{} \div 7 = 9$

MISSING FACTORS

Solve the problems by filling in the box with a number that will make the
math statement true.

1. ☐ ÷ 4 = 4

2. ☐ ÷ 4 = 6

3. ☐ ÷ 9 = 11

4. ☐ ÷ 5 = 7

5. ☐ ÷ 5 = 5

6. ☐ ÷ 12 = 11

7. ☐ ÷ 9 = 6

8. ☐ ÷ 8 = 3

9. ☐ ÷ 12 = 9

10. ☐ ÷ 6 = 6

11. ☐ ÷ 12 = 12

12. ☐ ÷ 12 = 2

13. ☐ ÷ 3 = 10

14. ☐ ÷ 7 = 6

15. ☐ ÷ 11 = 11

16. ☐ ÷ 7 = 8

17. ☐ ÷ 9 = 5

18. ☐ ÷ 8 = 4

19. ☐ ÷ 7 = 9

20. ☐ ÷ 12 = 4

21. ☐ ÷ 9 = 8

22. ☐ ÷ 12 = 6

23. ☐ ÷ 8 = 12

24. ☐ ÷ 5 = 11

25. ☐ ÷ 4 = 8

26. ☐ ÷ 8 = 10

27. ☐ ÷ 7 = 11

28. ☐ ÷ 12 = 5

29. ☐ ÷ 11 = 8

30. ☐ ÷ 7 = 10

Place Space

Hundred Thousand s	Ten Thousand s	One Thousand	Hundred s	Tens	Ones		Tentths	Hundredths
9	3	2 ,	4	8	6	.	1	7

1. Name the place value of the digit "4" in these numbers:

A. 3,**4**32 _____   B. **4**2,351 _____

C. **4**5 _____   D. **4**73,115 _____

E. 620.**4**8 _____   F. 50**4**.3 _____

G. 81.3**4** _____   H. 6**4**,332.5 _____

I. 888,**4**15 _____   J. 7**4**.3 _____

2. Tell which digit is in the tens place:

A. 1,536 _____   B. 53 _____

C. 47.2 _____   D. 504.6 _____

E. 8,346 _____   F. 416.8 _____

G. 902 _____   H. 52,374 _____

I. 357,618 _____   J. 495 _____

3. Tell which digit is in the tenths place:

A. 15.25 _____   B. 1.9 _____

C. 325.17 _____   D. 516.87 _____

E. 45.8 _____   F. 24.3 _____

G. 6.27 _____   H. 742.16 _____

I. 534.06 _____   J. 9,834.12 _____

Place Space

Hundred Thousand s	Ten Thousand s	One Thousand	Hundred s	Tens	Ones	Tentths	Hundredths
4	5	9	, 3	6	7 .	1	2

1. Name the place value of the digit "9" in these numbers:

A. 30**9** _____   B. 17,05**9** _____

C. 15**9**,342 _____   D. 475,**9**12 _____

E. **9**2,106 _____   F. 8.4**9** _____

G. **9**62 _____   H. 142.**9**5 _____

I. 5,89**6** _____   J. **9**,178 _____

2. Tell which digit is in the ones place:

A. 342 _____   B. 126 _____

C. 4,715 _____   D. 54,781 _____

E. 56,783 _____   F. 1,342.7 _____

G. 310.26 _____   H. 10.59 _____

I. 79 _____   J. 843.2 _____

3. Tell which digit is in the hundreds place:

A. 852 _____   B. 46,283 _____

C. 3,946.5 _____   D. 3,542.1 _____

E. 81,407 _____   F. 123,748 _____

G. 9,364.17 _____   H. 675 _____

I. 345,120 _____   J. 3,412.05 _____

Rounding Round-Up

To round any number, follow these simple rules:
Underline the place value you are rounding to.
Circle the digit to the right of the underlined digit.
If the circled number is 0, 1, 2, 3, or 4 the underlined digit stays the same.
If the circled number is 5, 6, 7, 8, or 9 the underlined digit goes up by 1.
The circled digit and all digits to the right become a zero.

1. Round these numbers to the nearest ten:

A. 42 _____ B. 554 _____
C. 87 _____ D. 436 _____
E. 133 _____ F. 3,771 _____
G. 289 _____ H. 408 _____
I. 1,415 _____ J. 1,982 _____

2. Round these numbers to the nearest hundred:

A. 3,288 _____ B. 551 _____
C. 768 _____ D. 381 _____
E. 1,349 _____ F. 675 _____
G. 156 _____ H. 7,245 _____
I. 8,337 _____ J. 2,819 _____

3. Round these numbers to the nearest thousand:

A. 4,670 _____ B. 46,667 _____
C. 3,099 _____ D. 3,501 _____
E. 61,389 _____ F. 23,748 _____
G. 9,364 _____ H. 2,651 _____
I. 215,189 _____ J. 3,712 _____

Rounding Round-Up

To round any number, follow these simple rules:
Underline the place value you are rounding to.
Circle the digit to the right of the underlined digit.
If the circled number is 0, 1, 2, 3, or 4 the underlined digit stays the same.
If the circled number is 5, 6, 7, 8, or 9 the underlined digit goes up by 1.
The circled digit and all digits to the right become a zero.

1. Round these numbers to the nearest hundred:

A. 646 _____   B. 867 _____

C. 172 _____   D. 759 _____

E. 345 _____   F. 3,498 _____

G. 581 _____   H. 735 _____

I. 1,293 _____   J. 1,611 _____

2. Round these numbers to the nearest thousand:

A. 3,397 _____   B. 5,551 _____

C. 1,768 _____   D. 8,381 _____

E. 4,349 _____   F. 12,675 _____

G. 7,156 _____   H. 7,245 _____

I. 18,337 _____   J. 2,719 _____

3. Round these numbers to the nearest tenth:

A. 12.84 _____   B. 176.94 _____

C. 304.46 _____   D. 22.38 _____

E. 88.13 _____   F. 5.26 _____

G. 749.82 _____   H. 36.76 _____

I. 8.57 _____   J. 9.31 _____

Rounding Round-Up

To round any number, follow these simple rules:
Underline the place value you are rounding to.
Circle the digit to the right of the underlined digit.
If the circled number is 0, 1, 2, 3, or 4 the underlined digit stays the same.
If the circled number is 5, 6, 7, 8, or 9 the underlined digit goes up by 1.
The circled digit and all digits to the right become a zero.

1. Round these numbers to the nearest hundred:

A. 1,442 _____ B. 426 _____

C. 839 _____ D. 854 _____

E. 4,562 _____ F. 3,396 _____

G. 339 _____ H. 40,491 _____

I. 881 _____ J. 1,816 _____

2. Round these numbers to the nearest thousand:

A. 38,815 _____ B. 6,587 _____

C. 5,446 _____ D. 14,318 _____

E. 7,227 _____ F. 5,672 _____

G. 4,980 _____ H. 9,194 _____

I. 11,392 _____ J. 43,488 _____

3. Round these numbers to the nearest ten thousand:

A. 24,170 _____ B. 47,127 _____

C. 55,099 _____ D. 83,591 _____

E. 62,989 _____ F. 26,748 _____

G. 19,764 _____ H. 92,651 _____

I. 217,105 _____ J. 138,712 _____

Decimal Dimensions

A. Write each fraction as a decimal:

1. $\frac{32}{100}$ _____

2. $\frac{9}{10}$ _____

3. $\frac{48}{100}$ _____

4. $\frac{7}{100}$ _____

5. $\frac{1}{10}$ _____

6. $\frac{5}{10}$ _____

7. $\frac{23}{100}$ _____

8. $\frac{6}{100}$ _____

9. $\frac{95}{100}$ _____

10. $\frac{14}{100}$ _____

B. Write each decimal as a fraction:

1. 0.5 _____

2. 0.31 _____

3. 0.48 _____

4. 0.4 _____

5. 0.08 _____

6. 0.8 _____

7. 0.3 _____

8. 0.24 _____

9. 0.7 _____

10. 0.56 _____

C. Write each expression as a fraction and a decimal:

1. six tenths _____

2. four hundredths _____

Decimal Dimensions

A. Write each mixed number as a decimal:

$5\dfrac{6}{10}$ _____ $7\dfrac{8}{10}$ _____

$42\dfrac{3}{100}$ _____ $13\dfrac{13}{100}$ _____

$71\dfrac{3}{10}$ _____ $5\dfrac{81}{100}$ _____

$4\dfrac{8}{100}$ _____ $14\dfrac{2}{100}$ _____

$1\dfrac{1}{100}$ _____ $3\dfrac{3}{10}$ _____

B. Write each decimal as a fraction:

1. 3.52 _____   **6.** 4.09 _____

2. 27.09 _____   **7.** 70.2 _____

3. 5.1 _____   **8.** 12.17 _____

4. 30.25 _____   **9.** 5.18 _____

5. 12.04 _____   **10.** 1.4 _____

C. Write each expression as a fraction and a decimal:

1. seven and one tenth _____

2. ninety and four hundredths _____

What Is Next?

Find the pattern in each series below. Write the next three members of the series on the lines. Write the pattern rule (+ or - and number).

1. 5, 10, 15, 20, 25, 30,   **35**   **40**   **45**
    Rule: **+ 5** _____

2. 18, 16, 14, 12, 10,   ___   ___   ___
    Rule: _____

3. 3, 6, 9, 12, 15,   ___   ___   ___
    Rule: _____

4. 100, 94, 88, 82, 76,   ___   ___   ___
    Rule: _____

5. 240, 250, 260, 270, 280,   ___   ___   ___
    Rule: _____

6. 3,500, 3,400, 3,300, 3,200,   ___   ___   ___
    Rule: _____

7. 12, 24, 36, 48, 60, 72,   ___   ___   ___
    Rule: _____

8. 80, 72, 64, 56, 48, 40,   ___   ___   ___
    Rule: _____

9. 11, 22, 33, 44, 55, 66,   ___   ___   ___
    Rule: _____

10. 4, 8, 12, 16, 20, 24,   ___   ___   ___
    Rule: _____

Bonus: Design your own pattern for your class to solve.

What Is Next?

Find the pattern in each series below. Write the next three members
of the series on the lines. Write the pattern rule (+ or - and number).

1.   5,   10,   15,   20,   25,   30,   **35   40   45**
  Rule: + 5 _____   ___ ___ ___

2.   111,   112,   113,   114,   115,
  Rule: _____   ___ ___ ___

3.   125,   120,   115,   110,   105,
  Rule: _____   ___ ___ ___

4.   28,   35,   42,   49,   56,
  Rule: _____   ___ ___ ___

5.   12,   23,   34,   45,   56,
  Rule: _____   ___ ___ ___

6.   78,   75,   72,   69,   66,
  Rule: _____   ___ ___ ___

7.   1,300,   1,250,   1,200,   1,150,
  Rule: _____   ___ ___ ___

8.   88,   98,   108,   118,   128,
  Rule: _____   ___ ___ ___

9.   10,   25,   40,   55,   70,   85,
  Rule: _____   ___ ___ ___

10.   210,   180,   150,   120,   90,
  Rule: _____   ___ ___ ___

Bonus: Design your own pattern for your class to solve.

Picture Perfect

Look at the pictures below. Shade in the parts to show the fraction named. Remember, the number of shaded parts goes on the top and the total number of parts goes on the bottom.

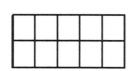

$$\frac{7}{10}$$

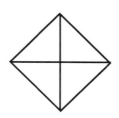

$$\frac{1}{4}$$

$$\frac{5}{8}$$

$$\frac{4}{9}$$

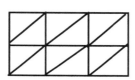

$$\frac{9}{12}$$

$$\frac{3}{8}$$

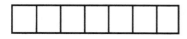

$$\frac{3}{7}$$

$$\frac{5}{6}$$

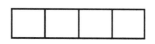

$$\frac{3}{4}$$

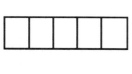

$$\frac{3}{5}$$

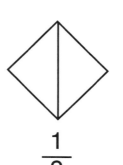

$$\frac{1}{2}$$

$$\frac{4}{10}$$

Picture Perfect

Look at the fractions in each pair. Name the equal fractions.

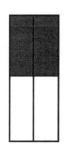 

$\dfrac{2}{4}$ = _____

 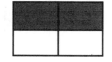

_____ = _____

_____ = _____

_____ = _____

 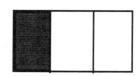

_____ = _____

 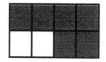

_____ = _____

_____ = _____

_____ = _____

CD-3723

Compare Squares

Write a fraction to name the shaded parts for each figure. Write >, <, or = for each pair.

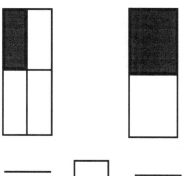

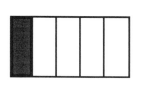 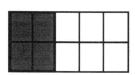

____ ▢ ____

____ ▢ ____

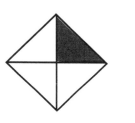 

____ ▢ ____

____ ▢ ____

____ ▢ ____

____ ▢ ____

____ ▢ ____

____ ▢ ____

Perimeter

Find the perimeter of each shape by adding the measurement of each side.

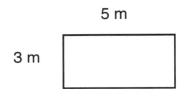

5 m

3 m

Perimeter = ‗‗‗‗‗‗‗‗

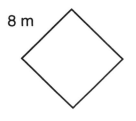

8 m

Perimeter = ‗‗‗‗‗‗‗‗

12 m

6 m

Perimeter = ‗‗‗‗‗‗‗‗

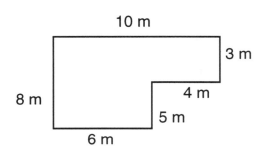

10 m

3 m

8 m

4 m

5 m

6 m

Perimeter = ‗‗‗‗‗‗‗‗

6 m

4 m

Perimeter = ‗‗‗‗‗‗‗‗

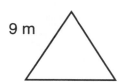

9 m

Perimeter = ‗‗‗‗‗‗‗‗

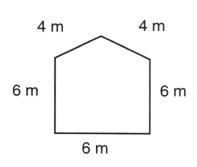

4 m   4 m

6 m   6 m

6 m

Perimeter = ‗‗‗‗‗‗‗‗

Words Into Math

Animals	
TIGERS	✔✔✔✔✔
MONKEYS	✔✔✔✔✔✔✔✔
KANGAROOS	✔
ELEPHANTS	✔✔✔✔✔
ZEBRAS	✔✔✔

Mrs. Lopez's 3rd grade class was very excited about their field trip to the zoo. The class voted to find out which animals they liked the best. Each checkmark shows one child's vote.

1. Which animal did the most of the class like best?

_____

2. How many children voted?

_____

3. How many more students liked the tigers better than the zebras?

_____

4. How many students wanted to see the kangaroo?

_____

5. Which two animals got the same number of votes?

_____

6. How many votes did the tigers and monkeys get?

_____

7. All the boys voted for the tigers and the elephants. How many boys are in Mrs. Lopez's class?

_____

8. How many children liked the monkeys best?

_____

9. Mrs. Lopez made name tags for all the children. How many name tags did she make?

_____

10. How many votes for the zebras, elephants, and kangaroos?

_____

Words Into Math

ACTIVITY	STARTING TIME
Band Practice	2:45 PM
Football Practice	3:00 PM
Cheerleading Practice	2:45 PM
Ecology Club Meeting	2:40 PM
Honors Club Meeting	2:50 PM
Chorus Practice	3:30 PM

City State High School has this schedule posted. It names all of the after school activities for clubs and sports groups. It also gives the time each one starts.

1. What time does cheerleading practice begin?

_____

2. What time does band practice begin?

_____

3. Which two activities start at the same time?

_____

4. Football begins at 3:00. How much later before chorus begins ?

_____

5. How many minutes between the time band and football practice starts?

_____

6. Chorus practice ends at 5:00. How long is practice?

_____

7. Which starts earlier, Honors Club or band practice?

_____

8. Football practice ends at 5 PM. How long does practice last?

_____

9. Matt was 10 minutes late for Honors Club. What time did he get there?

_____

10. Can Joe go to band practice and the ecology club meeting?

_____

Words Into Math

FOOD	VOTES
Tacos	★★★
Chicken Nuggets	★★★★★
Pizza	★★★★★★★★
Hot Dog	★★★★
Hamburger	★★★★★
Spaghetti	★★★★★★

One day each week a class at school votes on what food will be served on "free day". This week the third graders voted. This chart shows how they voted. Each star stands for five votes.

1. How many children voted for tacos on free day?

_____

2. Which food got the most votes for free day?

_____

3. How many children voted for spaghetti?

_____

4. Did more children vote for hot dogs or hamburgers ?

_____

5. Which two foods got the same number of votes?

_____

6. How many votes did pizza get?

_____

7. Which food got 20 votes?

_____

8. Which food got the fewest votes?

_____

9. How many students voted this week?

_____

10. How many students voted for chicken, pizza, and tacos all together?

_____

Words Into Math

MENU	
Cheeseburger	$2.00
Hamburger	$1.90
French Fries	$ .85
Soda	$ .70
Milk Shake	$1.25
Ice Cream	$ .95

Mr. Smith's third grade class stopped at Burger Bonanza to eat lunch during their field trip last week. This is the menu the children had to choose from.

1. How much does a milk shake cost?

_____

2. What item costs more than anything else on the menu?

_____

3. How much more does a cheeseburger cost than a hamburger?

_____

4. Which costs more, a milk shake or hamburger?

_____

5. How much do french fries and a soda cost all together?

_____

6. Chris ate his lunch and he had 80 ¢ left. Could he buy anything else?

_____

7. How much do a hamburger, fries, and ice cream cost?

_____

8. Lisa ordered a hamburger and a milk shake. How much did she spend?

_____

9. Hallie had $5.00. Could she buy a cheeseburger, fries, and a milk shake?

_____

10. Shelia has $3.00. Can she buy a cheeseburger and milk shake?

_____

Words Into Math

Read the paragraph carefully then answer the questions.

There are some really good players on Jamal's Little League baseball team . For the first five games, Sam got 11 hits. Javier got 9 hits. Charlie has had 4 hits. There are still 3 games left to play this season.

1. How many hits have Javier and Sam gotten together?

_____

2. Who got more hits, Charlie or Javier?

_____

3. Jamal got three times as many hits as Javier. How many hits did Jamal get?

_____

4. How many games will the boys play this season?

_____

5. Who got more hits, Sam or Charlie?

_____

6. How many hits have Javier, Sam, and Charlie gotten all together?

_____

7. Charlie had 8 hits less than Greg. How many hits did Greg get?

_____

8. How many hits did Javier and Charlie get together?

_____

Skills Evaluation

Choose the best answer to these review questions.
Circle the correct answer.

1. Add: 3,442
        + 4,258
 	
   A. 7,690   B. 7,600
 	
   C. 6,700   D. 7,700
	2. Subtract: 1,862
	            - 785
	
	   A. 1,123 B. 1,077
	
	   C. 1,177 D. 1,083

3. Subtract: 5,040
           - 3,639
 	
   A. 2,619   B. 1,301
 	
   C. 1,419   D. 1,401
	4. Multiply: 12×11
	
	   A. 121 B. 120
	
	   C. 132 D. 123

5. Which of these facts is <u>not</u> correct?
 	
A. $6 \times 9 = 54$ B. $12 \times 10 = 121$
 	
C. $9 \times 7 = 63$ D. $5 \times 8 = 40$
	6. Which problem does not have a product of 24?
	
	   A. 12×2 B. 3×8
	
	   C. 4×5 D. 6×4

7. Which of the multiplication facts is correct?
 	
A. $11 \times 10 = 111$ B. $12 \times 7 = 84$
 	
C. $7 \times 8 = 54$ D. $8 \times 8 = 81$
	8. Solve: $4 \times 9 \div 6 = \square$
	
	    A. 12 B. 36
	
	    C. 6 D. 8

9. Find the missing factor:
      $27 \div \square = 9$
 	
   A. 4   B. 3
 	
   C. 7   D. 2
	10. Find the missing factor:
	      $72 \div \square = 8$
	
	   A. 12 B. 7
	
	   C. 8 D. 9

Skills Evaluation

Choose the best answer to these review questions.
Circle the correct answer.

---

1. Find the missing factor:
$$96 \div \square = 12$$

   A. 7   B. 8

   C. 9   D. 10

2. Find the missing factor:
$$55 \div \square = 5$$

   A. 8   B. 9

   C. 10   D. 11

---

3. The number is 157,236. The 3 is in which place?

A. ones   B. tens

C. hundreds   D. thousands

4. The number is 30,521. The 3 is in which place?

A. tens   B. hundreds

C. thousands   D. ten thousands

---

5. The number is 13,987. The 3 is in which place?

A. ones   B. tens

C. hundreds   D. thousands

6. The number is 25,376. The 3 is in which place?

A. tens   B. hundreds

C. thousands   D. ten thousands

---

7. Round to the nearest ten:
461

   A. 462   B. 460

   C. 470   D. 500

8. Round to the nearest hundred:
1,548

   A. 1,550   B. 1,540

   C. 1,500   D. 1,600

---

9. Round to the nearest hundred:
691

   A. 1,000   B. 690

   C. 680   D. 700

10. Round to the nearest thousand:
15,820

   A. 15,000   B. 15,800

   C. 15,900   D. 16,000

           CD-3723

Name _____

Skills Evaluation

Choose the best answer to these review questions.
Circle the correct answer.

---

1. Tell if the expression is <, >, or =.

$$12 \times 3 \,\square\, 6 \times 6$$

A. >   B. <

C. =

2. Tell if the expression is <, >, or =.

$$64 \div 8 \,\square\, 3 \times 4$$

A. >   B. <

C. =

---

3. Tell if the expression is <, >, or =.

$$9 \times 5 \,\square\, 8 \times 6$$

A. >   B. <

C. =

4. Tell if the expression is <, >, or =.

$$72 \div 8 \,\square\, 5 \times 2$$

A. >   B. <

C. =

---

5. Write the fraction as a decimal:

$$\frac{3}{10}$$

A. 3.1   B. .310

C. .3   D. .03

6. Write the fraction as a decimal:

$$\frac{14}{100}$$

A. .014   B. .14

C. 1.4   D. 14.0

---

7. Multiply: 543
                     x   4

A. 2,172   B. 2,167

C. 201,612   D. 2,062

8. Multiply: 372
                     x   6

A. 181,412   B. 2,222

C. 2,232   D. 1,038

---

9. Which fraction is shown?

A. 3/5   B. 3/6

C. 3/8   D. 5/8

10. Which fraction is shown?

A. 7/3   B. 3/10

C. 7/10   D. 8/10

Math Whiz!

_____

receives this award for

_____

Keep up the great work!

_____   _____

signed   date

Dazzling Division!

_____

receives this award for

_____

Keep up the dazzling work!

_____   _____

signed   date

Multiplication Award

_____

receives this award for

_____

Keep up the great work!

_____ _____

signed   date

Place Value Superstar!

_____

is a Place Value Superstar!

_____

You are terrific!

_____ _____

signed   date

103   CD-3723

Answer Key

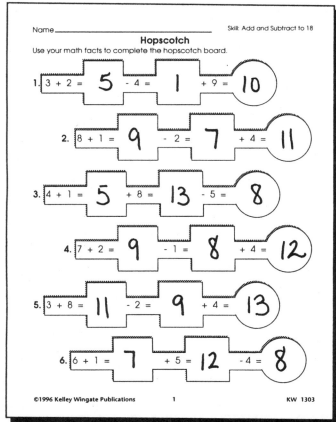

Name_____   Skill: Add and Subtract to 18

Hopscotch
Use your math facts to complete the hopscotch board.

1. 3 + 2 = **5**   - 4 = **1**   + 9 = **10**

2. 8 + 1 = **9**   - 2 = **7**   + 4 = **11**

3. 4 + 1 = **5**   + 8 = **13**   - 5 = **8**

4. 7 + 2 = **9**   - 1 = **8**   + 4 = **12**

5. 3 + 8 = **11**   - 2 = **9**   + 4 = **13**

6. 6 + 1 = **7**   + 5 = **12**   - 4 = **8**

©1996 Kelley Wingate Publications   1   KW 1303

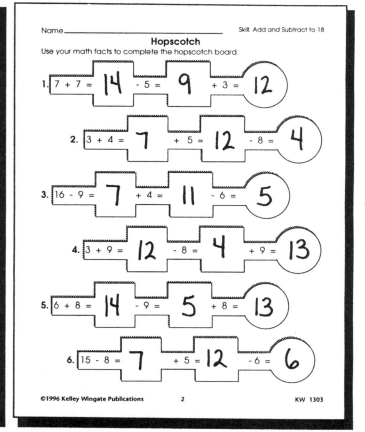

Name_____   Skill: Add and Subtract to 18

Hopscotch
Use your math facts to complete the hopscotch board.

1. 7 + 7 = **14**   - 5 = **9**   + 3 = **12**

2. 3 + 4 = **7**   + 5 = **12**   - 8 = **4**

3. 16 - 9 = **7**   + 4 = **11**   - 6 = **5**

4. 3 + 9 = **12**   - 8 = **4**   + 9 = **13**

5. 6 + 8 = **14**   - 9 = **5**   + 8 = **13**

6. 15 - 8 = **7**   + 5 = **12**   - 6 = **6**

©1996 Kelley Wingate Publications   2   KW 1303

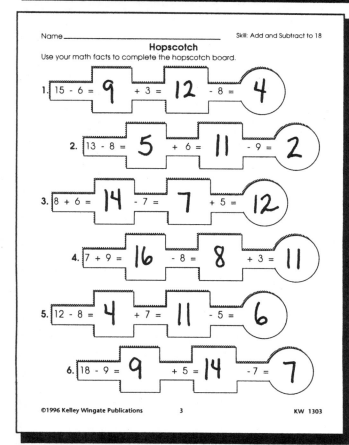

Name_____   Skill: Add and Subtract to 18

Hopscotch
Use your math facts to complete the hopscotch board.

1. 15 - 6 = **9**   + 3 = **12**   - 8 = **4**

2. 13 - 8 = **5**   + 6 = **11**   - 9 = **2**

3. 8 + 6 = **14**   - 7 = **7**   + 5 = **12**

4. 7 + 9 = **16**   - 8 = **8**   + 3 = **11**

5. 12 - 8 = **4**   + 7 = **11**   - 5 = **6**

6. 18 - 9 = **9**   + 5 = **14**   - 7 = **7**

©1996 Kelley Wingate Publications   3   KW 1303

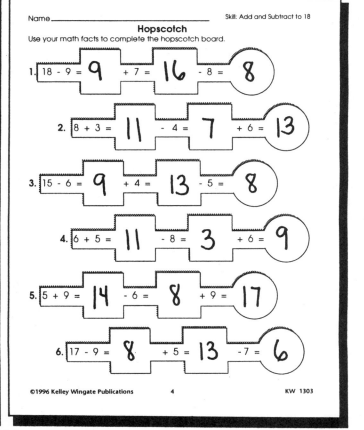

Name_____   Skill: Add and Subtract to 18

Hopscotch
Use your math facts to complete the hopscotch board.

1. 18 - 9 = **9**   + 7 = **16**   - 8 = **8**

2. 8 + 3 = **11**   - 4 = **7**   + 6 = **13**

3. 15 - 6 = **9**   + 4 = **13**   - 5 = **8**

4. 6 + 5 = **11**   - 8 = **3**   + 6 = **9**

5. 5 + 9 = **14**   - 6 = **8**   + 9 = **17**

6. 17 - 9 = **8**   + 5 = **13**   - 7 = **6**

©1996 Kelley Wingate Publications   4   KW 1303

       CD-3723

Answer Key

Name_____ Skill: Add and Subtract to 18

Compare Squares

Compare the number sentences. Write <, >, or = in the square to make a true math statement. The first problem is done for you.

1. 3 + 6 [<] 7 + 4
2. 18 - 9 [>] 13 - 5
3. 5 + 8 [<] 9 + 6
4. 13 - 4 [=] 12 - 3
5. 6 + 6 [>] 9 + 2
6. 16 - 8 [<] 11 - 2
7. 7 + 8 [>] 9 + 5
8. 15 - 9 [<] 12 - 5
9. 14 - 6 [>] 11 - 4
10. 7 + 6 [=] 4 + 9
11. 15 - 7 [>] 13 - 8
12. 5 + 9 [>] 6 + 7
13. 7 + 9 [<] 8 + 9
14. 12 - 4 [<] 8 + 4
15. 7 + 5 [>] 15 - 6
16. 18 - 9 [<] 6 + 5
17. 5 + 9 [<] 8 + 8
18. 17 - 9 [<] 3 + 6
19. 8 + 7 [>] 9 + 5
20. 13 - 6 [<] 6 + 4

© 1996 Kelley Wingate Publications   5   KW 1303

Name_____ Skill: Add and Subtract to 18

Compare Squares

Compare the number sentences. Write >, <, or = in the square to make a true math statement. The first problem is done for you.

1. 6 + 4 [<] 9 + 2
2. 14 - 8 [<] 17 - 9
3. 8 + 5 [<] 9 + 6
4. 7 + 4 [=] 6 + 5
5. 6 + 8 [>] 9 + 4
6. 12 - 3 [>] 14 - 6
7. 7 + 9 [=] 8 + 8
8. 15 - 7 [>] 16 - 9
9. 14 - 7 [<] 12 - 4
10. 13 - 5 [=] 17 - 9
11. 6 + 6 [>] 9 + 2
12. 16 - 7 [>] 12 - 5
13. 3 + 8 [<] 9 + 4
14. 16 - 8 [<] 6 + 3
15. 17 - 8 [<] 8 + 2
16. 4 + 8 [=] 6 + 6
17. 12 - 9 [<] 13 - 5
18. 8 + 9 [>] 6 + 7
19. 13 - 7 [<] 4 + 4
20. 8 + 7 [>] 16 - 9

© 1996 Kelley Wingate Publications   6   KW 1303

Name_____ Skill: Add and Subtract to 18

Compare Squares

Compare the number sentences. Write <, >, or = in the square to make a true math statement. The first problem is done for you.

1. 3 + 7 - 5 [<] 2 + 2 + 2
2. 18 - 9 + 3 [>] 5 + 8 - 4
3. 4 + 8 - 3 [<] 17 - 9 + 2
4. 12 - 4 + 6 [>] 9 + 6 - 8
5. 4 + 5 + 6 [>] 3 + 6 + 5
6. 11 - 4 - 3 [<] 8 + 3 - 6
7. 5 + 3 + 8 [<] 12 - 4 + 9
8. 14 - 6 + 2 [=] 11 - 8 + 7
9. 3 + 8 - 6 [<] 2 + 7 - 3
10. 15 - 8 + 4 [<] 2 + 4 + 6
11. 9 + 4 - 5 [<] 15 - 6 + 2
12. 13 - 6 + 4 [<] 5 + 4 + 3
13. 15 - 6 - 2 [=] 4 + 6 - 3
14. 9 + 2 - 5 [<] 8 - 4 + 5
15. 7 + 5 - 6 [=] 3 + 3 - 0
16. 14 - 6 + 3 [>] 9 + 5 - 4
17. 12 - 9 + 7 [=] 17 - 9 + 2
18. 8 + 1 - 4 [<] 15 - 7 + 1
19. 3 + 7 + 7 [<] 4 + 8 + 6
20. 3 + 4 - 2 [=] 6 + 3 - 4

© 1996 Kelley Wingate Publications   7   KW 1303

Name_____ Skill: Add and Subtract to 18

Compare Squares

Compare the number sentences. Write <, >, or = in the square to make a true math statement. The first problem is done for you.

1. 5 + 8 - 4 [<] 13 - 6 + 3
2. 15 - 6 - 5 [>] 18 - 9 - 8
3. 4 + 8 + 3 [>] 12 - 6 + 8
4. 12 - 7 - 1 [<] 5 + 6 - 4
5. 13 - 6 + 7 [>] 7 + 2 + 3
6. 8 + 5 - 4 [<] 15 - 6 + 3
7. 9 + 8 - 7 [>] 8 + 4 - 3
8. 16 - 8 + 7 [<] 7 + 2 + 9
9. 12 - 9 + 8 [<] 15 - 9 + 6
10. 4 + 4 + 4 [>] 5 + 8 - 4
11. 14 - 5 + 8 [>] 16 - 9 + 7
12. 5 + 7 - 4 [>] 8 + 6 - 7
13. 15 - 8 - 6 [<] 13 - 5 + 8
14. 5 + 4 + 8 [=] 2 + 6 + 9
15. 16 - 9 + 4 [<] 12 - 4 + 5
16. 16 - 7 + 4 [>] 7 + 5 - 3
17. 16 - 9 + 5 [=] 13 - 5 + 4
18. 18 - 9 - 6 [<] 15 - 7 - 4
19. 5 + 7 + 5 [<] 4 + 5 + 9
20. 13 - 8 + 5 [<] 8 + 6 - 3

© 1996 Kelley Wingate Publications   8   KW 1303

Leapfrog (page 9)

Name _____ Skill: Add and Subtract to 18

Leapfrog
Use your math facts to move across the lily pads.

1. 3 + 6 = ⟨9⟩ - 4 = ⟨5⟩
2. 7 + 8 = ⟨15⟩ - 9 = ⟨6⟩
3. 17 - 9 = ⟨8⟩ + 8 = ⟨16⟩
4. 9 + 3 = ⟨12⟩ - 6 = ⟨6⟩
5. 14 - 8 = ⟨6⟩ + 7 = ⟨13⟩
6. 12 - 3 = ⟨9⟩ + 4 = ⟨13⟩
7. 5 + 6 = ⟨11⟩ - 7 = ⟨4⟩
8. 15 - 7 = ⟨8⟩ + 3 = ⟨11⟩
9. 7 + 9 = ⟨16⟩ - 8 = ⟨8⟩
10. 13 - 5 = ⟨8⟩ + 9 = ⟨17⟩

Bonus

16
−
8
[8]
+
9
[17]
+
1
[18]

© 1996 Kelley Wingate Publications   9   KW 1303

Leapfrog (page 10)

Name _____ Skill: Add and Subtract to 18

Leapfrog
Use your math facts to move across the lily pads.

1. 12 - 6 = ⟨6⟩ + 4 = ⟨10⟩
2. 15 - 9 = ⟨6⟩ + 8 = ⟨14⟩
3. 9 + 4 = ⟨13⟩ - 6 = ⟨7⟩
4. 11 - 3 = ⟨8⟩ + 7 = ⟨15⟩
5. 14 - 8 = ⟨6⟩ + 9 = ⟨15⟩
6. 7 + 7 = ⟨14⟩ - 5 = ⟨9⟩
7. 5 + 8 = ⟨13⟩ - 4 = ⟨9⟩
8. 12 - 5 = ⟨7⟩ + 8 = ⟨15⟩
9. 2 + 9 = ⟨11⟩ - 4 = ⟨7⟩
10. 13 - 4 = ⟨9⟩ + 9 = ⟨18⟩

Bonus

6
+
7
[13]
−
8
[5]
+
9
[14]

© 1996 Kelley Wingate Publications   10   KW 1303

Blankety-Blanks (page 11)

Name _____ Skill: Add and Subtract to 18

Blankety- Blanks
Solve the problems below and write the answer in the box. On the blanket,
shade in all the numbers that are in the answer boxes.
The answers will make a pattern.

5 + 7 - 4 = [8]
5 + 5 - 7 = [3]
4 + 5 + 9 = [18]
2 + 7 - 8 = [1]
4 + 7 - 5 = [6]
15 - 8 + 3 = [10]
12 - 3 + 8 = [17]
5 + 9 - 7 = [7]
8 + 8 - 7 = [9]
14 - 9 + 8 = [13]
9 + 3 - 7 = [5]
14 - 9 + 7 = [12]
10 - 3 + 8 = [15]
13 - 9 + 7 = [11]
2 + 6 + 8 = [16]
15 - 8 + 7 = [14]

11	3	12	18
0	4	7	19
14	21	20	25
21	23	5	4
17	19	30	0
20	27	9	21
16	2	31	26
33	0	6	19
12	24	22	20
13	10	15	8

© 1996 Kelley Wingate Publications   11   KW 1303

Blankety-Blanks (page 12)

Name _____ Skill: Add and Subtract to 18

Blankety- Blanks
Solve the problems below and write the answer in the box. On the blanket,
shade in all the numbers that are in the answer boxes.
The answers will make a pattern.

4 + 7 - 5 = [6]
15 - 6 + 8 = [17]
3 + 4 + 9 = [16]
18 - 9 + 3 = [12]
15 - 9 + 2 = [8]
14 - 7 + 4 = [11]
16 - 8 + 7 = [15]
7 + 8 - 6 = [9]
12 - 3 + 9 = [18]
11 - 4 + 3 = [10]
13 - 5 - 4 = [4]
17 - 9 + 5 = [13]
7 + 6 - 8 = [5]
16 - 7 + 5 = [14]
3 + 8 - 4 = [7]
14 - 5 - 6 = [3]

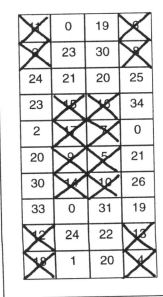

11	0	19	8
8	23	30	9
24	21	20	25
23	18	16	34
2	17	14	0
20	9	5	21
30	14	10	26
33	0	31	19
12	24	22	13
18	1	20	4

© 1996 Kelley Wingate Publications   12   KW 1303

Answer Key

Skill: Addition Regrouping

Name _____

Regrouping
Add the following problems. Do not forget to regroup when necessary.

52 +19 = 71	36 +84 = 120	85 +46 = 131	17 +55 = 72	43 +29 = 72	36 +38 = 74	25 +68 = 93	49 +19 = 68
59 +28 = 87	22 +57 = 79	46 +39 = 85	23 +37 = 60	55 +28 = 83	65 +26 = 91	79 +17 = 96	44 +27 = 71
53 +38 = 91	36 +39 = 75	26 +47 = 73	37 +44 = 81	48 +19 = 67	39 +28 = 67	69 +22 = 91	47 +24 = 71
77 +16 = 93	38 +58 = 96	56 +29 = 85	27 +37 = 64	45 +38 = 83	29 +61 = 90	53 +29 = 82	37 +28 = 65

48 + 23 = 71   26 + 39 = 65   46 + 27 = 73   36 + 16 = 52
46 + 35 = 81   77 + 15 = 92   48 + 27 = 75   17 + 54 = 71
38 + 38 = 76   52 + 29 = 81   35 + 27 = 62   44 + 36 = 80
61 + 29 = 90   36 + 46 = 82   34 + 28 = 62   53 + 27 = 80
68 + 28 = 96   47 + 23 = 70   67 + 29 = 96   39 + 48 = 87

© 1996 Kelley Wingate Publications   13   KW 1303

Skill: Addition Regrouping

Name _____

Regrouping
Add the following problems. Do not forget to regroup when necessary.

17 +75 = 92	28 +37 = 65	55 +19 = 74	34 +46 = 80	57 +33 = 90	38 +45 = 83	24 +46 = 70
79 +22 = 101	34 +77 = 111	35 +67 = 102	65 +48 = 113	55 +78 = 133	64 +66 = 130	49 +62 = 111
452 +238 = 690	243 +139 = 382	786 +145 = 931	689 +149 = 838	576 +235 = 811	779 +160 = 939	389 +421 = 810
570 +145 = 715	223 +499 = 722	696 +216 = 912	338 +377 = 715	589 +147 = 736	248 +388 = 636	199 +559 = 758

69 + 53 = 122   27 + 85 = 112   49 + 71 = 120
35 + 66 = 101   36 + 89 = 125   55 + 45 = 100
48 + 92 = 140   77 + 34 = 111   96 + 38 = 134
57 + 49 = 106   85 + 77 = 162   60 + 82 = 142
193 + 268 = 461   284 + 346 = 630   356 + 475 = 831

© 1996 Kelley Wingate Publications   14   KW 1303

Skill: Addition Regrouping

Name _____

Regrouping
Add the following problems. Do not forget to regroup when necessary.

3,123 +4,938 = 8,061	3,142 +3,859 = 7,001	6,522 +1,479 = 8,001	4,657 +1,393 = 6,050	3,826 +4,575 = 8,401
5,777 +2,633 = 8,410	3,575 +2,437 = 6,012	6,259 +1,853 = 8,112	2,474 +2,787 = 5,261	7,389 +1,622 = 9,011
2,842 +1,658 = 4,500	5,486 +1,526 = 7,012	3,389 +4,949 = 8,338	4,576 +1,545 = 6,121	3,974 +4,148 = 8,122
3,773 +1,648 = 5,421	2,196 +3,916 = 6,112	6,438 +2,777 = 9,215	5,719 +1,284 = 7,003	2,399 +2,139 = 4,538

1,269 + 4,153 = 5,422   2,427 + 5,285 = 7,712
3,179 + 1,471 = 4,650   3,235 + 2,966 = 6,201
5,436 + 1,589 = 7,025   4,556 + 2,458 = 7,014
6,358 + 1,942 = 8,300   4,377 + 2,624 = 7,001
2,845 + 1,676 = 4,521   3,156 + 4,855 = 8,011

© 1996 Kelley Wingate Publications   15   KW 1303

Skill: Subtraction With Regrouping

Name _____

Regrouping
Subtract the following problems. Do not forget to regroup when necessary.

40 -29 = 11	38 -19 = 19	42 -16 = 26	87 -39 = 48	74 -15 = 59	93 -74 = 19	84 -35 = 49	66 -48 = 18
52 -24 = 28	46 -28 = 18	72 -53 = 19	61 -28 = 33	67 -38 = 29	54 -36 = 18	92 -73 = 19	75 -28 = 47
58 -39 = 19	53 -29 = 24	81 -32 = 49	92 -59 = 33	71 -64 = 7	71 -32 = 39	93 -76 = 17	54 -39 = 15
73 -25 = 48	95 -48 = 47	84 -27 = 57	64 -39 = 25	83 -28 = 55	43 -34 = 9	52 -47 = 5	81 -27 = 54

47 - 18 = 29   41 - 25 = 16   84 - 47 = 37   75 - 46 = 29
86 - 39 = 47   55 - 17 = 38   61 - 12 = 49   71 - 34 = 37
34 - 18 = 16   62 - 49 = 13   75 - 17 = 58   43 - 38 = 5
73 - 38 = 35   94 - 66 = 28   86 - 58 = 28   56 - 49 = 7
44 - 15 = 29   42 - 28 = 14   96 - 29 = 67   91 - 56 = 35

© 1996 Kelley Wingate Publications   16   KW 1303

Answer Key

© 1996 Kelley Wingate Publications

Worksheet 17

Name _____ Skill: Subtraction Regrouping

Regrouping
Subtract the following problems. Do not forget to regroup when necessary.

326	972	438	371	407	738	954
- 285	- 689	- 259	- 296	- 138	- 199	- 466
41	**283**	**179**	**75**	**269**	**539**	**488**

529	514	625	560	522	464	743
- 262	- 407	- 467	- 382	- 278	- 267	- 166
267	**107**	**168**	**178**	**244**	**197**	**577**

632	643	586	257	416	371	814
- 238	- 439	- 197	- 149	- 187	- 184	- 465
394	**204**	**389**	**108**	**229**	**187**	**349**

774	323	486	634	811	635	642
- 189	- 199	- 397	- 277	- 347	- 498	- 299
585	**124**	**89**	**357**	**464**	**137**	**343**

222 - 153 = **69**   423 - 285 = **138**   843 - 477 = **366**

435 - 166 = **269**   536 - 189 = **347**   415 - 248 = **167**

628 - 199 = **429**   317 - 128 = **189**   347 - 188 = **159**

757 - 179 = **578**   632 - 377 = **255**   431 - 382 = **49**

673 - 388 = **285**   754 - 686 = **68**   956 - 587 = **369**

Worksheet 18

Name _____ Skill: Subtraction Regrouping

Regrouping
Subtract the following problems. Do not forget to regroup when necessary.

3,246	4,318	3,741	7,358	9,534
- 2,685	- 2,529	- 2,962	- 1,979	- 4,696
561	**1,789**	**779**	**5,379**	**4,838**

5,269	6,125	5,622	4,264	7,143
- 2,682	- 3,467	- 3,826	- 2,678	- 1,667
2,587	**2,658**	**1,796**	**1,586**	**5,476**

4,632	5,386	2,537	3,171	8,514
- 2,938	- 1,497	- 1,849	- 1,284	- 4,865
1,694	**3,889**	**688**	**1,887**	**3,649**

7,732	4,386	6,234	6,351	6,742
- 6,984	- 3,977	- 4,277	- 4,498	- 2,995
748	**409**	**1,957**	**1,853**	**3,747**

2,422 - 1,543 = **879**   6,423 - 3,585 = **2,838**

8,436 - 4,778 = **3,658**   4,135 - 1,647 = **2,488**

5,362 - 4,969 = **393**   3,415 - 2,548 = **867**

6,728 - 1,999 = **4,729**   3,127 - 1,288 = **1,839**

3,347 - 1,688 = **1,659**   5,123 - 3,694 = **1,429**

Worksheet 19

Name _____ Skill: Subtraction Regrouping

Regrouping
Subtract the following problems. Do not forget to regroup when necessary.

30	70	80	70	40	70	60	80
- 17	- 49	- 59	- 46	- 32	- 31	- 27	- 59
13	**21**	**21**	**24**	**8**	**39**	**33**	**21**

50	40	60	60	50	60	90	70
- 34	- 29	- 48	- 18	- 38	- 56	- 57	- 28
16	**11**	**12**	**42**	**12**	**4**	**33**	**42**

60	50	80	90	70	70	90	50
- 28	- 44	- 65	- 59	- 17	- 52	- 71	- 29
32	**6**	**15**	**31**	**53**	**18**	**19**	**21**

70	90	80	60	80	40	50	30
- 35	- 88	- 23	- 28	- 57	- 32	- 48	- 12
35	**2**	**57**	**32**	**23**	**8**	**2**	**18**

20 - 18 = **2**   40 - 25 = **15**   80 - 47 = **33**   70 - 46 = **24**

80 - 39 = **41**   50 - 17 = **33**   60 - 12 = **48**   70 - 34 = **36**

30 - 18 = **12**   60 - 49 = **11**   70 - 17 = **53**   40 - 38 = **2**

70 - 38 = **32**   90 - 66 = **24**   80 - 58 = **22**   50 - 49 = **1**

40 - 15 = **25**   40 - 28 = **12**   90 - 29 = **61**   90 - 56 = **34**

Worksheet 20

Name _____ Skill: Subtraction Regrouping

Regrouping
Subtract the following problems. Do not forget to regroup when necessary.

306	970	408	300	407	730	900
- 214	- 389	- 159	- 196	- 125	- 506	- 466
92	**581**	**249**	**104**	**282**	**224**	**434**

509	510	605	500	520	404	700
- 352	- 287	- 582	- 356	- 288	- 367	- 546
157	**223**	**23**	**144**	**232**	**37**	**154**

602	640	506	200	410	801	800
- 136	- 479	- 192	- 123	- 381	- 354	- 645
466	**161**	**314**	**77**	**29**	**447**	**155**

707	120	406	600	810	605	600
- 529	- 106	- 179	- 257	- 446	- 528	- 328
178	**14**	**227**	**343**	**364**	**77**	**272**

202 - 135 = **67**   420 - 258 = **162**   800 - 367 = **433**

405 - 116 = **289**   530 - 198 = **332**   400 - 284 = **116**

608 - 149 = **459**   310 - 182 = **128**   300 - 125 = **175**

707 - 198 = **509**   630 - 458 = **172**   400 - 328 = **72**

603 - 324 = **279**   750 - 268 = **482**   900 - 578 = **322**

Answer Key

Sheet 1 (page 21)

Name _____ Skill: Subtraction Regrouping

Regrouping

Subtract the following problems. Do not forget to regroup when necessary.

3,540	6,307	3,041	7,300	9,000
- 2,865	- 2,639	- 2,692	- 4,897	- 4,569
675	**3,668**	**349**	**2,403**	**4,431**

5,260	6,105	5,022	4,200	7,000
- 3,852	- 4,479	- 3,745	- 1,522	- 4,523
1,408	**1,626**	**1,277**	**2,678**	**2,477**

4,630	5,306	2,037	3,100	8,000
- 3,841	- 2,827	- 1,958	- 2,247	- 5,724
789	**2,479**	**79**	**853**	**2,276**

7,730	4,306	6,034	6,300	6,000
- 3,852	- 1,977	- 2,699	- 1,432	- 5,116
3,878	**2,329**	**3,335**	**4,868**	**884**

2,420 - 1,683 = **737**   6,203 - 4,384 = **1,819**

9,200 - 7,746 = **1,454**   4,000 - 2,674 = **1,326**

5,630 - 4,652 = **978**   3,504 - 2,845 = **659**

6,700 - 3,611 = **3,089**   3,000 - 1,828 = **1,172**

4,330 - 1,841 = **2,489**   7,100 - 3,546 = **3,554**

© 1996 Kelley Wingate Publications   21   KW 1303

Sheet 2 (page 22)

Name _____ Skill: Multiplication Facts

Beat the Clock

How quickly can you complete this page? Time yourself. Ready, set, go!

Time : _____

Number Correct : _____

2	2	2	2	2	2	2	2
x 3	x 1	x 11	x 8	x 0	x 5	x 2	x 10
6	**2**	**22**	**16**	**0**	**10**	**4**	**20**

2	2	2	2	2	2	2	2
x 7	x 4	x 9	x 12	x 6	x 4	x 1	x 3
14	**8**	**18**	**24**	**12**	**8**	**2**	**6**

6	7	3	2	8	11	0	1
x 2	x 2	x 2	x 2	x 2	x 2	x 2	x 2
12	**14**	**6**	**4**	**16**	**22**	**0**	**2**

9	12	5	6	10	4	7	3
x 2	x 2	x 2	x 2	x 2	x 2	x 2	x 2
18	**24**	**10**	**12**	**20**	**8**	**14**	**6**

9 x 2 = **18**   7 x 2 = **14**   4 x 2 = **8**   3 x 2 = **6**   6 x 2 = **12**

5 x 2 = **10**   8 x 2 = **16**   7 x 2 = **14**   9 x 2 = **18**   2 x 2 = **4**

0 x 2 = **0**   3 x 2 = **6**   8 x 2 = **16**   5 x 2 = **10**   6 x 2 = **12**

2 x 7 = **14**   2 x 1 = **2**   2 x 5 = **10**   2 x 2 = **4**   2 x 9 = **18**

10 x 2 = **20**   12 x 2 = **24**   11 x 2 = **22**   7 x 2 = **14**   4 x 2 = **8**

© 1996 Kelley Wingate Publications   22   KW 1303

Sheet 3 (page 23)

Name _____ Skill: Multiplication Facts

Beat the Clock

How quickly can you complete this page? Time yourself. Ready, set, go!

Time : _____

Number Correct : _____

2	5	1	0	4	3	6	9
x 3	x 3	x 3	x 3	x 3	x 3	x 3	x 3
6	**15**	**3**	**0**	**12**	**9**	**18**	**27**

11	7	10	8	5	6	2	4
x 3	x 3	x 3	x 3	x 3	x 3	x 3	x 3
33	**21**	**30**	**24**	**15**	**18**	**6**	**12**

3	3	3	3	3	3	3	3
x 5	x 4	x 3	x 9	x 11	x 1	x 6	x 10
15	**12**	**9**	**27**	**33**	**3**	**18**	**30**

3	3	3	3	3	3	3	3
x 2	x 12	x 0	x 7	x 8	x 4	x 3	x 9
6	**36**	**0**	**21**	**24**	**12**	**9**	**27**

9 x 3 = **27**   7 x 3 = **21**   4 x 3 = **12**   3 x 3 = **9**   6 x 3 = **18**

5 x 3 = **15**   8 x 3 = **24**   7 x 3 = **21**   9 x 3 = **27**   2 x 3 = **6**

3 x 2 = **6**   3 x 3 = **9**   3 x 8 = **24**   3 x 6 = **18**   3 x 0 = **0**

3 x 4 = **12**   3 x 1 = **3**   3 x 5 = **15**   3 x 9 = **27**   3 x 7 = **21**

10 x 3 = **30**   12 x 3 = **36**   11 x 3 = **33**   4 x 3 = **12**   6 x 3 = **18**

© 1996 Kelley Wingate Publications   23   KW 1303

Sheet 4 (page 24)

Name _____ Skill: Multiplication Facts

Beat the Clock

How quickly can you complete this page? Time yourself. Ready, set, go!

Time : _____

Number Correct : _____

4	4	4	4	4	4	4	4
x 3	x 5	x 9	x 10	x 0	x 6	x 4	x 7
12	**20**	**36**	**40**	**0**	**24**	**16**	**28**

4	4	4	4	4	4	4	4
x 2	x 8	x 7	x 11	x 1	x 12	x 3	x 9
8	**32**	**28**	**44**	**4**	**48**	**12**	**36**

6	7	3	2	10	4	5	11
x 4	x 4	x 4	x 4	x 4	x 4	x 4	x 4
24	**28**	**12**	**8**	**40**	**16**	**20**	**44**

0	8	9	12	1	4	7	2
x 4	x 4	x 4	x 4	x 4	x 4	x 4	x 4
0	**32**	**36**	**48**	**4**	**16**	**28**	**8**

9 x 4 = **36**   7 x 4 = **28**   4 x 4 = **16**   3 x 4 = **12**   6 x 4 = **24**

5 x 4 = **20**   8 x 4 = **32**   1 x 4 = **4**   0 x 4 = **0**   2 x 4 = **8**

4 x 2 = **8**   4 x 3 = **12**   4 x 8 = **32**   4 x 6 = **24**   4 x 0 = **0**

4 x 4 = **16**   4 x 1 = **4**   4 x 5 = **20**   4 x 7 = **28**   4 x 9 = **36**

10 x 4 = **40**   12 x 4 = **48**   11 x 4 = **44**   4 x 4 = **16**   8 x 4 = **32**

© 1996 Kelley Wingate Publications   24   KW 1303

Answer Key

Worksheet 1 (page 25)

Name _____   Skill: Multiplication Facts

Beat the Clock

How quickly can you complete this page? Time yourself. Ready, set, go!

Time : _____

Number Correct : _____

5 x3	5 x5	5 x9	5 x10	5 x7	5 x0	5 x6	5 x1
15	25	45	50	35	0	30	5

5 x2	5 x8	5 x4	5 x11	5 x1	5 x12	5 x3	5 x5
10	40	20	55	5	60	15	25

6 x5	7 x5	3 x5	12 x5	0 x5	5 x5	2 x5	11 x5
30	35	15	60	0	25	10	55

9 x5	4 x5	8 x5	10 x5	1 x5	3 x5	7 x5	6 x5
45	20	40	50	5	15	35	30

9 x 5 = 45   7 x 5 = 35   4 x 5 = 20   3 x 5 = 15   6 x 5 = 30
5 x 5 = 25   8 x 5 = 40   0 x 5 = 0   1 x 5 = 5   2 x 5 = 10
5 x 2 = 10   5 x 3 = 15   5 x 8 = 40   5 x 6 = 30   5 x 0 = 0
5 x 4 = 20   5 x 7 = 35   5 x 5 = 25   5 x 9 = 45   5 x 1 = 5
10 x 5 = 50   11 x 5 = 55   10 x 5 = 50   7 x 5 = 35   4 x 5 = 20

Worksheet 2 (page 26)

Name _____   Skill: Multiplication Facts

Beat the Clock

How quickly can you complete this page? Time yourself. Ready, set, go!

Time : _____

Number Correct : _____

6 x3	6 x5	6 x9	6 x0	6 x10	6 x7	6 x11	6 x1
18	30	54	0	60	42	66	6

6 x2	6 x8	6 x12	6 x1	6 x4	6 x6	6 x3	6 x5
12	48	72	6	24	36	18	30

6 x6	7 x6	3 x6	2 x6	11 x6	5 x6	12 x6	1 x6
36	42	18	12	66	30	72	6

9 x6	8 x6	10 x6	0 x6	1 x6	4 x6	5 x6	3 x6
54	48	60	0	6	24	30	18

1 x 6 = 6   7 x 6 = 42   4 x 6 = 24   3 x 6 = 18   6 x 6 = 36
5 x 6 = 30   8 x 6 = 48   0 x 6 = 0   9 x 6 = 54   2 x 6 = 12
6 x 7 = 42   6 x 3 = 18   6 x 8 = 48   6 x 6 = 36   6 x 0 = 0
6 x 4 = 24   6 x 9 = 54   6 x 5 = 30   6 x 2 = 12   6 x 1 = 6
10 x 6 = 60   12 x 6 = 72   11 x 6 = 66   7 x 6 = 42   3 x 6 = 18

Worksheet 3 (page 27)

Name _____   Skill: Multiplication Facts

Beat the Clock

How quickly can you complete this page? Time yourself. Ready, set, go!

Time : _____

Number Correct : _____

7 x3	7 x5	7 x11	7 x5	7 x10	7 x4	7 x7	7 x9
21	35	77	35	70	28	49	63

7 x2	7 x8	7 x0	7 x1	7 x12	7 x6	7 x3	7 x8
14	56	0	7	84	42	21	56

6 x7	7 x7	4 x7	2 x7	12 x7	8 x7	3 x7	11 x7
42	49	28	14	84	56	21	77

9 x7	0 x7	8 x7	5 x7	1 x7	10 x7	7 x7	1 x7
63	0	56	35	7	70	49	7

1 x 7 = 7   7 x 7 = 49   4 x 7 = 28   3 x 7 = 21   6 x 7 = 42
5 x 7 = 35   8 x 7 = 56   0 x 7 = 0   9 x 7 = 63   2 x 7 = 14
7 x 7 = 49   7 x 3 = 21   7 x 8 = 56   7 x 6 = 42   7 x 0 = 0
7 x 4 = 28   7 x 9 = 63   7 x 5 = 35   7 x 2 = 14   7 x 1 = 7
11 x 7 = 77   10 x 7 = 70   12 x 7 = 84   7 x 7 = 49   4 x 7 = 28

Worksheet 4 (page 28)

Name _____   Skill: Multiplication Facts

Beat the Clock

How quickly can you complete this page? Time yourself. Ready, set, go!

Time : _____

Number Correct : _____

8 x3	8 x5	8 x9	8 x4	8 x11	8 x0	8 x7	8 x9
24	40	72	32	88	0	56	72

8 x2	8 x8	8 x12	8 x1	8 x10	8 x6	8 x3	8 x5
16	64	96	8	80	48	24	40

10 x8	5 x8	12 x8	2 x8	3 x8	7 x8	6 x8	0 x8
80	40	96	16	24	56	48	0

9 x8	11 x8	8 x8	6 x8	1 x8	4 x8	5 x8	7 x8
72	88	64	48	8	32	40	56

5 x 8 = 40   1 x 8 = 8   4 x 8 = 32   3 x 8 = 24   6 x 8 = 48
0 x 8 = 0   8 x 8 = 64   7 x 8 = 56   9 x 8 = 72   2 x 8 = 16
8 x 9 = 72   8 x 3 = 24   8 x 8 = 64   8 x 6 = 48   8 x 0 = 0
8 x 4 = 32   8 x 7 = 56   8 x 5 = 40   8 x 2 = 16   8 x 1 = 8
11 x 8 = 88   10 x 8 = 80   12 x 8 = 96   3 x 8 = 24   9 x 8 = 72

Answer Key

Worksheet 29

Name _____ Skill: Multiplication Facts
Beat the Clock
How quickly can you complete this page? Time yourself. Ready, set, go!
Time : _____
Number Correct : _____

9 x12 = 108	9 x10 = 90	9 x9 = 81	9 x5 = 45	9 x3 = 27	9 x11 = 99	9 x4 = 36	9 x0 = 0
9 x7 = 63	9 x8 = 72	9 x2 = 18	9 x1 = 9	9 x4 = 36	9 x6 = 54	9 x3 = 27	9 x8 = 72
0 x9 = 0	7 x9 = 63	3 x9 = 27	2 x9 = 18	12 x9 = 108	5 x9 = 45	10 x9 = 90	1 x9 = 9
9 x9 = 81	11 x9 = 99	8 x9 = 72	6 x9 = 54	1 x9 = 9	4 x9 = 36	7 x9 = 63	3 x9 = 27

9 x 9 = 81   7 x 9 = 63   4 x 9 = 36   3 x 9 = 27   6 x 9 = 54
5 x 9 = 45   8 x 9 = 72   0 x 9 = 0   1 x 9 = 9   2 x 9 = 18
9 x 9 = 81   9 x 3 = 27   9 x 8 = 72   9 x 6 = 54   9 x 0 = 0
9 x 4 = 36   9 x 7 = 63   9 x 5 = 45   9 x 2 = 18   9 x 1 = 9
1 x 9 = 9   0 x 9 = 0   11 x 9 = 99   12 x 9 = 108   10 x 9 = 90

Worksheet 30

Name _____ Skill: Multiplication Facts
Beat the Clock
How quickly can you complete this page? Time yourself. Ready, set, go!
Time : _____
Number Correct : _____

10 x3 = 30	10 x5 = 50	10 x9 = 90	10 x5 = 50	10 x0 = 0	10 x7 = 70	10 x11 = 110	10 x9 = 90
10 x2 = 20	10 x8 = 80	10 x10 = 100	10 x1 = 10	10 x6 = 60	10 x4 = 40	10 x12 = 120	10 x2 = 20
11 x10 = 110	7 x10 = 70	3 x10 = 30	2 x10 = 20	5 x10 = 50	10 x10 = 100	12 x10 = 120	7 x10 = 70
9 x10 = 90	0 x10 = 0	8 x10 = 80	6 x10 = 60	1 x10 = 10	4 x10 = 40	5 x10 = 50	9 x10 = 90

8 x 10 = 80   0 x 10 = 0   4 x 10 = 40   3 x 10 = 30   6 x 10 = 60
5 x 10 = 50   1 x 10 = 10   7 x 10 = 70   9 x 10 = 90   2 x 10 = 20
10 x 9 = 90   10 x 3 = 30   10 x 8 = 80   10 x 6 = 60   10 x 0 = 0
10 x 4 = 40   10 x 1 = 10   10 x 5 = 50   10 x 2 = 20   10 x 7 = 70
10 x 6 = 60   10 x 0 = 0   10 x 10 = 100   10 x 11 = 110   10 x 12 = 120

Worksheet 31

Name _____ Skill: Multiplication Facts
Beat the Clock
How quickly can you complete this page? Time yourself. Ready, set, go!
Time : _____
Number Correct : _____

11 x3 = 33	11 x5 = 55	11 x9 = 99	11 x10 = 110	11 x12 = 132	11 x0 = 0	11 x6 = 66	11 x9 = 99
11 x2 = 22	11 x8 = 88	11 x4 = 44	11 x1 = 11	11 x7 = 77	11 x6 = 66	11 x11 = 121	11 x2 = 22
6 x11 = 66	0 x11 = 0	3 x11 = 33	2 x11 = 22	7 x11 = 77	5 x11 = 55	12 x11 = 132	6 x11 = 66
9 x11 = 99	11 x11 = 121	8 x11 = 88	6 x11 = 66	1 x11 = 11	4 x11 = 44	10 x11 = 110	3 x11 = 33

9 x 11 = 99   7 x 11 = 77   4 x 11 = 44   3 x 11 = 33   6 x 11 = 66
5 x 11 = 55   8 x 11 = 88   7 x 11 = 77   9 x 11 = 99   2 x 11 = 22
11 x 2 = 22   11 x 3 = 33   11 x 8 = 88   11 x 6 = 66   11 x 0 = 0
11 x 4 = 44   11 x 1 = 11   11 x 5 = 55   11 x 2 = 22   11 x 1 = 11
11 x 6 = 66   11 x 0 = 0   11 x 10 = 110   11 x 12 = 132   11 x 11 = 121

Worksheet 32

Name _____ Skill: Multiplication Facts
Beat the Clock
How quickly can you complete this page? Time yourself. Ready, set, go!
Time : _____
Number Correct : _____

12 x3 = 36	12 x11 = 132	12 x0 = 0	12 x5 = 60	12 x10 = 120	12 x7 = 84	12 x6 = 72	12 x9 = 108
12 x2 = 24	12 x8 = 96	12 x4 = 48	12 x1 = 12	12 x12 = 144	12 x8 = 96	12 x3 = 36	12 x7 = 84
0 x12 = 0	10 x12 = 120	3 x12 = 36	2 x12 = 24	11 x12 = 132	7 x12 = 84	5 x12 = 60	6 x12 = 72
9 x12 = 108	8 x12 = 96	12 x12 = 144	6 x12 = 72	1 x12 = 12	4 x12 = 48	8 x12 = 96	3 x12 = 36

1 x 12 = 12   0 x 12 = 0   4 x 12 = 48   3 x 12 = 36   6 x 12 = 72
5 x 12 = 60   8 x 12 = 96   7 x 12 = 84   9 x 12 = 108   2 x 12 = 24
12 x 9 = 108   12 x 3 = 36   12 x 8 = 96   12 x 6 = 72   12 x 0 = 0
12 x 4 = 48   12 x 7 = 84   12 x 5 = 60   12 x 2 = 24   12 x 1 = 12
12 x 6 = 72   12 x 0 = 0   12 x 10 = 120   12 x 12 = 144   12 x 11 = 132

Answer Key

Worksheet 33

9 ×3 = 27	4 ×7 = 28	3 ×8 = 24	9 ×9 = 81	6 ×6 = 36	3 ×6 = 18	5 ×6 = 30	2 ×8 = 16
5 ×8 = 40	7 ×2 = 14	5 ×5 = 25	8 ×6 = 48	2 ×9 = 18	5 ×3 = 15	9 ×0 = 0	7 ×6 = 42
9 ×7 = 63	8 ×9 = 72	5 ×4 = 20	7 ×8 = 56	9 ×4 = 36	5 ×7 = 35	4 ×6 = 24	1 ×8 = 8
6 ×2 = 12	7 ×7 = 49	9 ×6 = 54	3 ×7 = 21	8 ×8 = 64	2 ×8 = 16	5 ×9 = 45	1 ×7 = 7

9 x 3 = 27 7 x 5 = 35 4 x 9 = 36 3 x 6 = 18 6 x 7 = 42
5 x 5 = 25 8 x 2 = 16 7 x 4 = 28 9 x 7 = 63 8 x 4 = 32
9 x 2 = 18 3 x 8 = 24 8 x 8 = 64 6 x 6 = 36 6 x 9 = 54
8 x 4 = 32 8 x 9 = 72 8 x 5 = 40 2 x 8 = 16 9 x 5 = 45
1 x 6 = 6 0 x 0 = 0 4 x 6 = 24 7 x 2 = 14 4 x 3 = 12

© 1996 Kelley Wingate Publications   33   KW 1303

Worksheet 34

Name _____ Skill: Multiplication Facts
Multiplication Mania
How quickly can you complete this page? Time yourself. Ready, set, go!
Time: _____
Number Correct: _____

2 ×3 = 6	4 ×8 = 32	3 ×5 = 15	9 ×0 = 0	3 ×6 = 18	8 ×8 = 64	4 ×6 = 24	7 ×8 = 56
5 ×10 = 50	7 ×7 = 49	9 ×5 = 45	1 ×6 = 6	2 ×4 = 8	5 ×8 = 40	9 ×3 = 27	6 ×6 = 36
3 ×2 = 6	7 ×9 = 63	5 ×0 = 0	3 ×6 = 18	8 ×4 = 32	12 ×7 = 84	4 ×11 = 44	6 ×8 = 48
6 ×5 = 30	9 ×7 = 63	8 ×6 = 48	3 ×2 = 6	4 ×8 = 32	2 ×10 = 20	2 ×9 = 18	1 ×6 = 6

9 x 4 = 36 8 x 5 = 40 0 x 9 = 0 8 x 6 = 48 11 x 7 = 77
5 x 7 = 35 4 x 2 = 8 7 x 3 = 21 6 x 7 = 42 12 x 4 = 48
5 x 2 = 10 3 x 3 = 9 8 x 8 = 64 3 x 6 = 18 10 x 9 = 90
8 x 4 = 32 4 x 9 = 36 9 x 5 = 45 3 x 8 = 24 11 x 5 = 55
8 x 6 = 48 0 x 5 = 0 4 x 9 = 36 7 x 7 = 49 12 x 3 = 36

© 1996 Kelley Wingate Publications   34   KW 1303

Worksheet 35

Name _____ Skill: Multiplication Facts
Multiplication Mania
How quickly can you complete this page? Time yourself. Ready, set, go!
Time: _____
Number Correct: _____

12 ×3 = 36	4 ×8 = 32	3 ×11 = 33	9 ×0 = 0	5 ×7 = 35	10 ×2 = 20	8 ×1 = 8	2 ×8 = 16
5 ×10 = 50	7 ×9 = 63	12 ×6 = 72	8 ×8 = 64	4 ×9 = 36	7 ×11 = 77	12 ×10 = 120	7 ×6 = 42
6 ×7 = 42	8 ×5 = 40	6 ×4 = 24	4 ×3 = 12	9 ×7 = 63	5 ×3 = 15	4 ×6 = 24	1 ×8 = 8
8 ×2 = 16	7 ×4 = 28	11 ×6 = 66	3 ×10 = 30	8 ×4 = 32	2 ×9 = 18	5 ×7 = 35	1 ×7 = 7

9 x 4 = 36 7 x 8 = 56 7 x 9 = 63 3 x 3 = 9 6 x 6 = 36
5 x 6 = 30 4 x 2 = 8 5 x 4 = 20 4 x 7 = 28 8 x 8 = 64
9 x 9 = 81 3 x 11 = 33 8 x 6 = 48 6 x 10 = 60 3 x 9 = 27
4 x 4 = 16 6 x 3 = 18 9 x 5 = 45 2 x 8 = 16 8 x 5 = 40
5 x 6 = 30 0 x 10 = 0 4 x 6 = 24 7 x 7 = 49 4 x 3 = 12

© 1996 Kelley Wingate Publications   35   KW 1303

Worksheet 36

Name _____ Skill: Multiplication Facts
Multiplication Mania
How quickly can you complete this page? Time yourself. Ready, set, go!
Time: _____
Number Correct: _____

1 ×3 = 3	4 ×4 = 16	3 ×8 = 24	9 ×0 = 0	8 ×6 = 48	3 ×4 = 12	5 ×7 = 35	2 ×8 = 16
8 ×8 = 64	7 ×6 = 42	5 ×5 = 25	10 ×6 = 60	11 ×9 = 99	12 ×3 = 36	11 ×0 = 0	7 ×6 = 42
3 ×7 = 21	8 ×10 = 80	9 ×4 = 36	7 ×7 = 49	9 ×2 = 18	5 ×8 = 40	4 ×6 = 24	1 ×8 = 8
7 ×2 = 14	4 ×7 = 28	6 ×6 = 36	3 ×3 = 9	8 ×9 = 72	2 ×6 = 12	11 ×9 = 99	1 ×7 = 7

11 x 3 = 33 7 x 9 = 63 6 x 9 = 54 5 x 6 = 30 2 x 7 = 14
10 x 5 = 50 8 x 2 = 16 7 x 3 = 21 9 x 5 = 45 8 x 3 = 24
9 x 12 = 108 5 x 8 = 40 8 x 6 = 48 4 x 6 = 24 2 x 9 = 18
8 x 11 = 88 8 x 9 = 72 6 x 7 = 42 2 x 4 = 8 3 x 5 = 15
10 x 3 = 30 9 x 6 = 54 3 x 6 = 18 5 x 4 = 20 2 x 3 = 6

© 1996 Kelley Wingate Publications   36   KW 1303

Worksheet (page 37)

Name _____   Skill: Multiplication Facts

Compare Squares

Compare the number sentences. Write <, >, or = in the square to make a true math statement. The first problem is done for you.

1. 2 x 8 **<** 3 x 7
2. 3 x 4 **<** 2 x 7
3. 4 x 5 **>** 8 x 2
4. 3 x 9 **<** 4 x 7
5. 11 x 2 **<** 5 x 5
6. 3 x 3 **>** 2 x 4
7. 3 x 8 **=** 6 x 4
8. 8 x 2 **>** 3 x 5
9. 2 x 12 **=** 3 x 8
10. 5 x 3 **<** 4 x 4
11. 6 x 3 **=** 9 x 2
12. 2 x 7 **<** 5 x 3
13. 5 x 6 **<** 8 x 4
14. 7 x 4 **>** 3 x 8
15. 8 x 5 **<** 4 x 11
16. 6 x 8 **>** 5 x 9
17. 3 x 9 **>** 6 x 4
18. 8 x 7 **>** 9 x 6
19. 4 x 8 **<** 6 x 6
20. 10 x 5 **>** 7 x 7

© 1996 Kelley Wingate Publications   37   KW 1303

Worksheet (page 38)

Name _____   Skill: Multiplication Facts

Compare Squares

Compare the number sentences. Write <, >, or = in the square to make a true math statement. The first problem is done for you.

1. 5 x 4 **<** 7 x 3
2. 5 x 7 **<** 9 x 4
3. 6 x 5 **<** 8 x 4
4. 4 x 3 **=** 6 x 2
5. 7 x 4 **>** 9 x 3
6. 5 x 8 **=** 4 x 10
7. 6 x 7 **>** 5 x 5
8. 4 x 8 **<** 7 x 5
9. 6 x 6 **<** 5 x 8
10. 11 x 5 **<** 7 x 9
11. 6 x 5 **>** 4 x 7
12. 4 x 8 **<** 7 x 5
13. 4 x 4 **=** 2 x 8
14. 7 x 5 **<** 6 x 6
15. 6 x 7 **>** 8 x 3
16. 4 x 7 **<** 8 x 5
17. 9 x 6 **<** 7 x 8
18. 4 x 9 **=** 6 x 6
19. 5 x 5 **>** 7 x 3
20. 8 x 6 **>** 5 x 9

© 1996 Kelley Wingate Publications   38   KW 1303

Worksheet (page 39)

Name _____   Skill: Multiplication Facts

Compare Squares

Compare the number sentences. Write <, >, or = in the square to make a true math statement. The first problem is done for you.

1. 6 x 6 **<** 8 x 5
2. 9 x 12 **<** 10 x 11
3. 7 x 7 **<** 5 x 11
4. 12 x 4 **=** 8 x 6
5. 7 x 9 **<** 6 x 11
6. 5 x 9 **>** 6 x 7
7. 7 x 5 **<** 9 x 4
8. 9 x 6 **<** 8 x 8
9. 8 x 9 **=** 6 x 12
10. 6 x 5 **=** 10 x 3
11. 10 x 5 **<** 7 x 8
12. 5 x 12 **=** 10 x 6
13. 8 x 4 **>** 9 x 3
14. 6 x 7 **>** 8 x 5
15. 4 x 8 **<** 6 x 6
16. 10 x 7 **>** 11 x 6
17. 5 x 9 **<** 8 x 6
18. 7 x 4 **>** 3 x 6
19. 5 x 3 **<** 4 x 4
20. 10 x 4 **<** 6 x 7

© 1996 Kelley Wingate Publications   39   KW 1303

Worksheet (page 40)

Name _____   Skill: Multiplication Facts

Compare Squares

Compare the number sentences. Write <, >, or = in the square to make a true math statement. The first problem is done for you.

1. 9 x 4 **<** 7 x 6
2. 10 x 12 **<** 11 x 12
3. 9 x 5 **<** 6 x 8
4. 9 x 8 **=** 6 x 12
5. 8 x 8 **>** 7 x 9
6. 6 x 9 **<** 5 x 11
7. 12 x 5 **=** 6 x 10
8. 8 x 10 **<** 9 x 9
9. 4 x 9 **=** 3 x 12
10. 10 x 9 **<** 12 x 12
11. 8 x 7 **>** 10 x 5
12. 12 x 9 **<** 11 x 10
13. 11 x 5 **>** 8 x 6
14. 9 x 7 **<** 8 x 8
15. 7 x 10 **<** 8 x 9
16. 4 x 11 **>** 3 x 12
17. 6 x 10 **<** 8 x 9
18. 8 x 5 **=** 4 x 10
19. 5 x 7 **>** 3 x 11
20. 6 x 7 **<** 4 x 12

© 1996 Kelley Wingate Publications   40   KW 1303

Answer Key

MISSING FACTORS
Skill: Multiplication Facts

Name _____

Solve the problems by filling in the box with a number that will make the math statement true.

1. [4] x 4 = 16
2. [2] x 10 = 20
3. [8] x 3 = 24
4. [6] x 6 = 36
5. [7] x 5 = 35
6. [4] x 8 = 32
7. [9] x 2 = 18
8. [11] x 2 = 22
9. [4] x 7 = 28
10. [5] x 4 = 20
11. [4] x 9 = 36
12. [3] x 7 = 21
13. [5] x 6 = 30
14. [2] x 12 = 24
15. [3] x 11 = 33
16. [2] x 8 = 16
17. [4] x 6 = 24
18. [5] x 5 = 25
19. [9] x 3 = 27
20. [2] x 6 = 12
21. [2] x 4 = 8
22. [5] x 3 = 15
23. [3] x 3 = 9
24. [7] x 6 = 42
25. [7] x 7 = 49
26. [6] x 3 = 18
27. [3] x 8 = 24
28. [5] x 4 = 20
29. [5] x 7 = 35
30. [4] x 9 = 36

© 1996 Kelley Wingate Publications   41   KW 1303

MISSING FACTORS
Skill: Multiplication Facts

Name _____

Solve the problems by filling in the box with a number that will make the math statement true.

1. [3] x 7 = 21
2. [5] x 9 = 45
3. [3] x 12 = 36
4. [8] x 4 = 32
5. [5] x 3 = 15
6. [4] x 8 = 32
7. [9] x 7 = 63
8. [10] x 5 = 50
9. [8] x 7 = 56
10. [6] x 9 = 54
11. [5] x 7 = 35
12. [6] x 6 = 36
13. [4] x 12 = 48
14. [10] x 6 = 60
15. [12] x 7 = 84
16. [6] x 12 = 72
17. [4] x 7 = 28
18. [8] x 6 = 48
19. [12] x 5 = 60
20. [4] x 6 = 24
21. [9] x 6 = 54
22. [7] x 10 = 70
23. [3] x 4 = 12
24. [7] x 6 = 42
25. [5] x 8 = 40
26. [5] x 11 = 55
27. [8] x 7 = 56
28. [10] x 4 = 40
29. [9] x 9 = 81
30. [2] x 11 = 22

© 1996 Kelley Wingate Publications   42   KW 1303

MISSING FACTORS
Skill: Multiplication Facts

Name _____

Solve the problems by filling in the box with a number that will make the math statement true.

1. [12] x 3 = 36
2. [9] x 9 = 81
3. [8] x 9 = 72
4. [8] x 7 = 56
5. [8] x 8 = 64
6. [7] x 4 = 28
7. [2] x 10 = 20
8. [7] x 9 = 63
9. [8] x 5 = 40
10. [12] x 6 = 72
11. [6] x 3 = 18
12. [9] x 8 = 72
13. [9] x 4 = 36
14. [6] x 4 = 24
15. [5] x 4 = 20
16. [7] x 5 = 35
17. [6] x 10 = 60
18. [6] x 6 = 36
19. [9] x 2 = 18
20. [12] x 2 = 24
21. [5] x 12 = 60
22. [8] x 4 = 32
23. [10] x 4 = 40
24. [4] x 8 = 32
25. [9] x 7 = 63
26. [9] x 5 = 45
27. [8] x 11 = 88
28. [2] x 6 = 12
29. [12] x 2 = 24
30. [2] x 9 = 18

© 1996 Kelley Wingate Publications   43   KW 1303

MISSING FACTORS
Skill: Multiplication Facts

Name _____

Solve the problems by filling in the box with a number that will make the math statement true.

1. [8] x 7 = 56
2. [4] x 12 = 48
3. [5] x 9 = 45
4. [12] x 5 = 60
5. [9] x 9 = 81
6. [8] x 8 = 64
7. [4] x 4 = 16
8. [8] x 5 = 40
9. [9] x 3 = 27
10. [12] x 2 = 24
11. [6] x 6 = 36
12. [5] x 7 = 35
13. [9] x 5 = 45
14. [9] x 8 = 72
15. [12] x 7 = 84
16. [9] x 6 = 54
17. [12] x 8 = 96
18. [7] x 7 = 49
19. [12] x 6 = 72
20. [8] x 4 = 32
21. [12] x 12 = 144
22. [8] x 11 = 88
23. [9] x 12 = 108
24. [10] x 10 = 100
25. [10] x 12 = 120
26. [11] x 11 = 121
27. [12] x 11 = 132
28. [12] x 10 = 120
29. [8] x 12 = 96
30. [11] x 10 = 110

© 1996 Kelley Wingate Publications   44   KW 1303

Answer Key

Worksheet 1 (page 45)

Name _____

Skill: Multiplication Facts

Mystery Math

Look at the mystery number. Circle all math expressions in that row wich equal the mystery number. The first problem is done for you.

Mystery Number	Math Expression			
6	3 x 3	(6 x 1)	2 x 2	(3 x 2)
18	4 x 7	(2 x 9)	(3 x 6)	8 x 2
20	5 x 5	(10 x 2)	4 x 4	(5 x 4)
36	(3 x 12)	6 x 5	(4 x 9)	(6 x 6)
45	7 x 5	5 x 8	12 x 4	(9 x 5)
21	8 x 2	(3 x 7)	9 x 3	4 x 4
12	6 x 3	3 x 3	(2 x 6)	4 x 5
24	6 x 6	(8 x 3)	5 x 5	(2 x 12)
48	6 x 7	9 x 6	(8 x 6)	(4 x 12)

Worksheet 2 (page 46)

Name _____

Skill: Multiplication Facts

Mystery Math

Look at the mystery number. Circle all math expressions in that row wich equal the mystery number. The first problem is done for you.

Mystery Number	Math Expression			
8	3 x 3	(2 x 4)	6 x 2	(1 x 8)
25	8 x 3	6 x 4	(5 x 5)	2 x 11
12	(6 x 2)	3 x 3	(4 x 3)	(1 x 12)
42	12 x 4	(6 x 7)	8 x 6	(7 x 6)
60	(5 x 12)	12 x 6	8 x 8	(10 x 6)
27	(3 x 9)	4 x 7	3 x 8	7 x 3
32	12 x 4	(8 x 4)	11 x 3	6 x 5
56	12 x 4	6 x 9	(7 x 8)	9 x 5
54	12 x 4	(6 x 9)	7 x 8	9 x 5

Worksheet 3 (page 47)

Name _____

Skill: Multiplication Facts

Mystery Math

Look at the mystery number. Circle all math expressions in that row wich equal the mystery number. The first problem is done for you.

Mystery Number	Math Expression			
48	6 x 6	(12 x 4)	7 x 5	(6 x 8)
108	9 x 10	11 x 12	(12 x 9)	11 x 11
81	7 x 11	7 x 6	8 x 9	(9 x 9)
56	5 x 6	12 x 4	6 x 9	(8 x 7)
100	9 x 9	5 x 12	(10 x 10)	11 x 10
72	(12 x 6)	(9 x 8)	8 x 8	7 x 9
40	6 x 7	(8 x 5)	(10 x 4)	12 x 4
54	8 x 7	5 x 4	(6 x 9)	8 x 6
84	8 x 4	11 x 8	7 x 9	(7 x 12)

Worksheet 4 (page 48)

Name _____

Skill: Multiplication Facts

Mystery Math

Look at the mystery number. Circle all math expressions in that row wich equal the mystery number. The first problem is done for you.

Mystery Number	Math Expression			
144	12 x 11	(12 x 12)	11 x 11	4 x 4
120	11 x 11	11 x 12	10 x 11	(12 x 10)
60	(6 x 10)	12 x 6	6 x 11	(12 x 5)
121	12 x 11	11 x 10	(11 x 11)	10 x 12
56	6 x 9	8 x 8	9 x 7	(7 x 8)
132	12 x 12	12 x 13	(11 x 12)	11 x 11
110	11 x 11	(11 x 10)	11 x 12	11 x 11
72	12 x 7	(12 x 6)	(8 x 9)	9 x 9
96	11 x 6	12 x 9	9 x 11	(8 x 12)

Answer Key

Skill: Multiplication Facts

Leapfrog
Use your math facts to move across the lily pads.

1. 7 x 1 = (7) x 4 = (28)
2. 2 x 2 = (4) x 4 = (16)
3. 3 x 3 = (9) x 2 = (18)
4. 4 x 2 = (8) x 4 = (32)
5. 1 x 5 = (5) x 11 = (55)
6. 2 x 3 = (6) x 2 = (12)
7. 2 x 2 = (4) x 6 = (24)
8. 4 x 2 = (8) x 3 = (24)
9. 6 x 2 = (12) x 2 = (24)
10. 2 x 2 = (4) x 3 = (12)

Bonus

3
x
2
___
6
x
2
___
12
x
3
___
36

© 1996 Kelley Wingate Publications   49   KW 1303

Name _____

Skill: Multiplication Facts

Leapfrog
Use your math facts to move across the lily pads.

1. 4 x 3 = (12) x 5 = (60)
2. 2 x 4 = (8) x 8 = (64)
3. 3 x 2 = (6) x 4 = (24)
4. 2 x 2 = (4) x 3 = (12)
5. 4 x 2 = (8) x 4 = (32)
6. 1 x 3 = (3) x 6 = (18)
7. 4 x 0 = (0) x 5 = (0)
8. 3 x 2 = (6) x 7 = (42)
9. 5 x 2 = (10) x 6 = (60)
10. 3 x 4 = (12) x 7 = (84)

Bonus

1
x
5
___
5
x
2
___
10
x
6
___
60

© 1996 Kelley Wingate Publications   50   KW 1303

Name _____

Skill: Multiplication Facts

Leapfrog
Use your math facts to move across the lily pads.

1. 2 x 2 = (4) x 2 = (8)
2. 3 x 2 = (6) x 7 = (42)
3. 2 x 5 = (10) x 9 = (90)
4. 3 x 3 = (9) x 6 = (54)
5. 3 x 2 = (6) x 4 = (24)
6. 4 x 3 = (12) x 3 = (36)
7. 2 x 2 = (4) x 12 = (48)
8. 4 x 2 = (8) x 8 = (64)
9. 6 x 2 = (12) x 7 = (84)
10. 3 x 3 = (9) x 9 = (81)

Bonus

3
x
3
___
9
x
1
___
9
x
6
___
54

© 1996 Kelley Wingate Publications   51   KW 1303

Name _____

Skill: Multiplication Facts

Leapfrog
Use your math facts to move across the lily pads.

1. 2 x 3 = (6) x 5 = (30)
2. 4 x 2 = (8) x 6 = (48)
3. 2 x 5 = (10) x 11 = (110)
4. 2 x 2 = (4) x 7 = (28)
5. 3 x 3 = (9) x 12 = (108)
6. 4 x 3 = (12) x 4 = (48)
7. 2 x 4 = (8) x 7 = (56)
8. 6 x 2 = (12) x 12 = (144)
9. 3 x 3 = (9) x 8 = (72)
10. 2 x 3 = (6) x 7 = (42)

Bonus

2
x
2
___
4
x
2
___
8
x
9
___
72

© 1996 Kelley Wingate Publications   52   KW 1303

116

Answer Key

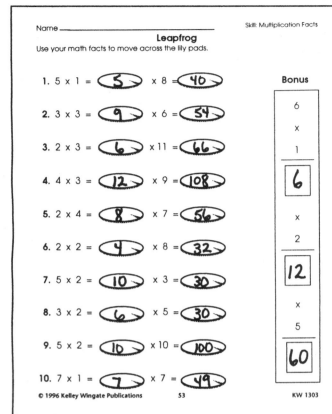

Name _____ Skill: Multiplication Facts
Leapfrog
Use your math facts to move across the lily pads.

1. 5 x 1 = ⬭5⬭ x 8 = ⬭40⬭
2. 3 x 3 = ⬭9⬭ x 6 = ⬭54⬭
3. 2 x 3 = ⬭6⬭ x 11 = ⬭66⬭
4. 4 x 3 = ⬭12⬭ x 9 = ⬭108⬭
5. 2 x 4 = ⬭8⬭ x 7 = ⬭56⬭
6. 2 x 2 = ⬭4⬭ x 8 = ⬭32⬭
7. 5 x 2 = ⬭10⬭ x 3 = ⬭30⬭
8. 3 x 2 = ⬭6⬭ x 5 = ⬭30⬭
9. 5 x 2 = ⬭10⬭ x 10 = ⬭100⬭
10. 7 x 1 = ⬭7⬭ x 7 = ⬭49⬭

Bonus

6
x
1
6
x
2
12
x
5
60

© 1996 Kelley Wingate Publications   53   KW 1303

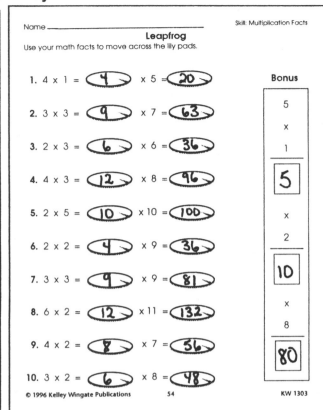

Name _____ Skill: Multiplication Facts
Leapfrog
Use your math facts to move across the lily pads.

1. 4 x 1 = ⬭4⬭ x 5 = ⬭20⬭
2. 3 x 3 = ⬭9⬭ x 7 = ⬭63⬭
3. 2 x 3 = ⬭6⬭ x 6 = ⬭36⬭
4. 4 x 3 = ⬭12⬭ x 8 = ⬭96⬭
5. 2 x 5 = ⬭10⬭ x 10 = ⬭100⬭
6. 2 x 2 = ⬭4⬭ x 9 = ⬭36⬭
7. 3 x 3 = ⬭9⬭ x 9 = ⬭81⬭
8. 6 x 2 = ⬭12⬭ x 11 = ⬭132⬭
9. 4 x 2 = ⬭8⬭ x 7 = ⬭56⬭
10. 3 x 2 = ⬭6⬭ x 8 = ⬭48⬭

Bonus

5
x
1
5
x
2
10
x
8
80

© 1996 Kelley Wingate Publications   54   KW 1303

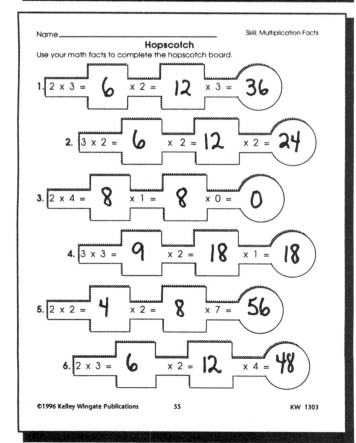

Name _____ Skill: Multiplication Facts
Hopscotch
Use your math facts to complete the hopscotch board.

1. 2 x 3 = **6** x 2 = **12** x 3 = **36**
2. 3 x 2 = **6** x 2 = **12** x 2 = **24**
3. 2 x 4 = **8** x 1 = **8** x 0 = **0**
4. 3 x 3 = **9** x 2 = **18** x 1 = **18**
5. 2 x 2 = **4** x 2 = **8** x 7 = **56**
6. 2 x 3 = **6** x 2 = **12** x 4 = **48**

©1996 Kelley Wingate Publications   55   KW 1303

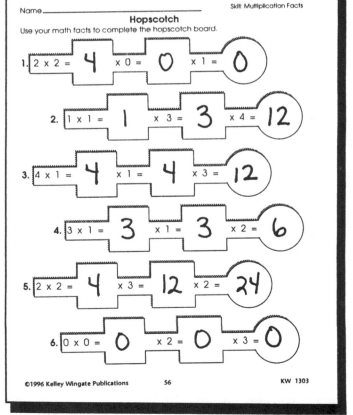

Name _____ Skill: Multiplication Facts
Hopscotch
Use your math facts to complete the hopscotch board.

1. 2 x 2 = **4** x 0 = **0** x 1 = **0**
2. 1 x 1 = **1** x 3 = **3** x 4 = **12**
3. 4 x 1 = **4** x 1 = **4** x 3 = **12**
4. 3 x 1 = **3** x 1 = **3** x 2 = **6**
5. 2 x 2 = **4** x 3 = **12** x 2 = **24**
6. 0 x 0 = **0** x 2 = **0** x 3 = **0**

©1996 Kelley Wingate Publications   56   KW 1303

Answer Key

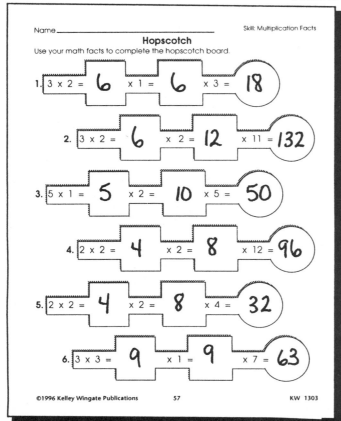

Hopscotch
Use your math facts to complete the hopscotch board.
Skill: Multiplication Facts

1. 3 x 2 = **6**   x 1 = **6**   x 3 = **18**
2. 3 x 2 = **6**   x 2 = **12**   x 11 = **132**
3. 5 x 1 = **5**   x 2 = **10**   x 5 = **50**
4. 2 x 2 = **4**   x 2 = **8**   x 12 = **96**
5. 2 x 2 = **4**   x 2 = **8**   x 4 = **32**
6. 3 x 3 = **9**   x 1 = **9**   x 7 = **63**

©1996 Kelley Wingate Publications   57   KW 1303

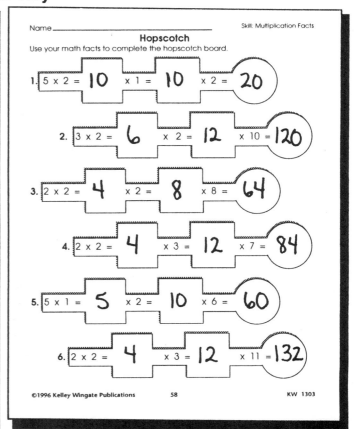

Name

Hopscotch
Use your math facts to complete the hopscotch board.
Skill: Multiplication Facts

1. 5 x 2 = **10**   x 1 = **10**   x 2 = **20**
2. 3 x 2 = **6**   x 2 = **12**   x 10 = **120**
3. 2 x 2 = **4**   x 2 = **8**   x 8 = **64**
4. 2 x 2 = **4**   x 3 = **12**   x 7 = **84**
5. 5 x 1 = **5**   x 2 = **10**   x 6 = **60**
6. 2 x 2 = **4**   x 3 = **12**   x 11 = **132**

©1996 Kelley Wingate Publications   58   KW 1303

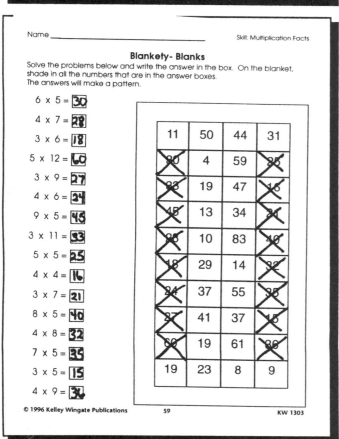

Name

Blankety- Blanks
Solve the problems below and write the answer in the box. On the blanket, shade in all the numbers that are in the answer boxes.
The answers will make a pattern.
Skill: Multiplication Facts

6 x 5 = **30**
4 x 7 = **28**
3 x 6 = **18**
5 x 12 = **60**
3 x 9 = **27**
4 x 6 = **24**
9 x 5 = **45**
3 x 11 = **33**
5 x 5 = **25**
4 x 4 = **16**
3 x 7 = **21**
8 x 5 = **40**
4 x 8 = **32**
7 x 5 = **35**
3 x 5 = **15**
4 x 9 = **36**

11	50	44	31
30	4	59	35
33	19	47	16
45	13	34	24
36	10	83	40
18	29	14	32
24	37	55	36
27	41	37	15
60	19	61	36
19	23	8	9

© 1996 Kelley Wingate Publications   59   KW 1303

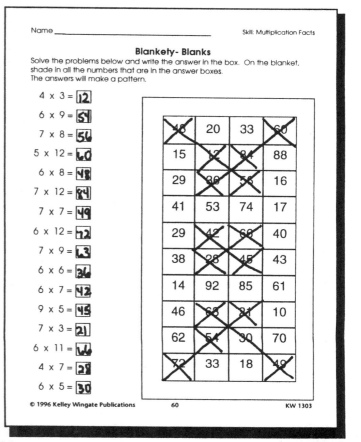

Name

Blankety- Blanks
Solve the problems below and write the answer in the box. On the blanket, shade in all the numbers that are in the answer boxes.
The answers will make a pattern.
Skill: Multiplication Facts

4 x 3 = **12**
6 x 9 = **54**
7 x 8 = **56**
5 x 12 = **60**
6 x 8 = **48**
7 x 12 = **84**
7 x 7 = **49**
6 x 12 = **72**
7 x 9 = **63**
6 x 6 = **36**
6 x 7 = **42**
9 x 5 = **45**
7 x 3 = **21**
6 x 11 = **66**
4 x 7 = **28**
6 x 5 = **30**

48	20	33	60
15	12	84	88
29	36	56	16
41	53	74	17
29	42	66	40
38	28	45	43
14	92	85	61
46	63	81	10
62	54	30	70
72	33	18	49

© 1996 Kelley Wingate Publications   60   KW 1303

Answer Key

Name _____

Skill: Multiplication Facts

Blankety- Blanks

Solve the problems below and write the answer in the box. On the blanket, shade in all the numbers that are in the answer boxes. The answers will make a pattern.

6 x 3 = **18**

9 x 12 = **108**

8 x 8 = **64**

10 x 12 = **120**

7 x 12 = **84**

10 x 6 = **60**

9 x 9 = **81**

10 x 11 = **110**

9 x 8 = **72**

7 x 9 = **63**

7 x 7 = **49**

8 x 12 = **96**

5 x 9 = **45**

9 x 6 = **54**

10 x 10 = **100**

7 x 8 = **56**

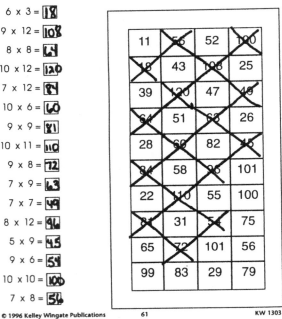

11	56	52	100
18	43	108	25
39	120	47	48
64	51	60	26
28	60	82	45
84	58	96	101
22	110	55	100
84	31	54	75
65	72	101	56
99	83	29	79

© 1996 Kelley Wingate Publications   61   KW 1303

Name _____

Skill: Multiplication Facts

Blankety- Blanks

Solve the problems below and write the answer in the box. On the blanket, shade in all the numbers that are in the answer boxes. The answers will make a pattern.

8 x 4 = **32**

6 x 12 = **72**

8 x 6 = **48**

10 x 12 = **120**

11 x 12 = **132**

7 x 6 = **42**

9 x 12 = **108**

11 x 11 = **121**

8 x 5 = **40**

4 x 9 = **36**

8 x 12 = **96**

7 x 9 = **63**

12 x 12 = **144**

9 x 9 = **81**

7 x 12 = **84**

10 x 10 = **100**

120	32	84	72
20	74	59	23
81	48	144	100
43	11	37	57
63	132	96	42
17	39	73	69
36	108	40	121
22	102	77	35
61	29	66	46
38	26	78	29

© 1996 Kelley Wingate Publications   62   KW 1303

Name _____

Skill: Multiplication Renaming

Renaming Multiplication Practice

Complete the problems below. Remember to rename numbers when needed.

15 x 5 **75**	26 x 3 **78**	18 x 4 **72**	12 x 9 **108**	27 x 2 **54**	22 x 5 **110**	32 x 4 **128**	41 x 5 **205**
23 x 3 **69**	19 x 5 **95**	37 x 3 **111**	16 x 7 **112**	71 x 6 **426**	54 x 2 **108**	33 x 4 **132**	28 x 3 **84**
43 x 9 **387**	51 x 7 **357**	36 x 8 **288**	84 x 4 **336**	21 x 6 **126**	33 x 7 **231**	56 x 3 **168**	62 x 4 **248**
39 x 2 **78**	28 x 6 **168**	52 x 4 **208**	67 x 5 **335**	41 x 8 **328**	34 x 9 **306**	18 x 5 **90**	23 x 6 **138**

6 x 12 = **72**   5 x 42 = **210**   4 x 75 = **300**   3 x 38 = **114**   7 x 44 = **308**

5 x 83 = **415**   8 x 32 = **256**   7 x 56 = **392**   9 x 18 = **162**   2 x 57 = **114**

22 x 9 = **198**   54 x 3 = **162**   73 x 8 = **584**   94 x 6 = **564**   45 x 3 = **135**

74 x 4 = **296**   58 x 7 = **406**   43 x 5 = **215**   98 x 2 = **196**   77 x 4 = **308**

56 x 6 = **336**   97 x 3 = **291**   84 x 6 = **504**   27 x 5 = **135**   51 x 9 = **459**

© 1996 Kelley Wingate Publications   63   KW 1303

Name _____

Skill: Multiplication Renaming

Renaming Multiplication Practice

Complete the problems below. Remember to rename numbers when needed.

42 x 5 **210**	46 x 6 **276**	37 x 7 **259**	32 x 8 **256**	54 x 2 **108**	67 x 3 **201**	84 x 4 **336**	73 x 5 **365**
37 x 4 **148**	52 x 3 **156**	75 x 2 **150**	49 x 5 **245**	63 x 7 **441**	51 x 8 **408**	44 x 7 **308**	29 x 4 **116**
123 x 4 **492**	315 x 2 **630**	182 x 5 **910**	143 x 3 **429**	224 x 4 **896**	615 x 6 **3,690**	428 x 3 **1,284**	423 x 2 **846**
129 x 4 **516**	217 x 3 **651**	318 x 7 **2,226**	456 x 5 **2,280**	185 x 8 **1,480**	277 x 4 **1,108**	189 x 5 **945**	323 x 6 **1,938**

6 x 123 = **738**   5 x 242 = **1,210**   4 x 375 = **1,500**   3 x 538 = **1,614**

5 x 383 = **1,915**   8 x 132 = **1,056**   7 x 456 = **3,192**   9 x 182 = **1,638**

222 x 9 = **1,998**   544 x 3 = **1,632**   732 x 8 = **5,856**   294 x 6 = **1,764**

574 x 4 = **2,296**   258 x 7 = **1,806**   643 x 5 = **3,215**   798 x 2 = **1,596**

256 x 6 = **1,536**   197 x 3 = **591**   484 x 6 = **2,904**   627 x 5 = **3,135**

© 1996 Kelley Wingate Publications   64   KW 1303

Answer Key

Name _____ Skill: Multiplication/Division

Leapfrog
Use your math facts to move across the lily pads.

1. 14 ÷ 2 = (7) x 3 = (21)
2. 3 x 12 = (36) ÷ 6 = (6)
3. 24 ÷ 6 = (4) x 8 = (32)
4. 30 ÷ 5 = (6) x 3 = (18)
5. 5 x 8 = (40) ÷ 4 = (10)
6. 18 ÷ 3 = (6) x 6 = (36)
7. 2 x 6 = (12) ÷ 3 = (4)
8. 16 ÷ 4 = (4) x 9 = (36)
9. 28 ÷ 4 = (7) x 5 = (35)
10. 8 x 3 = (24) ÷ 2 = (12)

Bonus

25
÷
5
[5]
x
4
[20]
÷
2
[10]

© 1996 Kelley Wingate Publications   65   KW 1303

Name _____ Skill: Multiplication/Division

Leapfrog
Use your math facts to move across the lily pads.

1. 40 ÷ 4 = (10) x 5 = (50)
2. 64 ÷ 8 = (8) x 7 = (56)
3. 5 x 4 = (20) ÷ 10 = (2)
4. 6 x 8 = (48) ÷ 4 = (12)
5. 72 ÷ 8 = (9) x 5 = (45)
6. 24 ÷ 4 = (6) x 9 = (54)
7. 6 x 6 = (36) ÷ 4 = (9)
8. 56 ÷ 7 = (8) x 4 = (32)
9. 5 x 12 = (60) ÷ 6 = (10)
10. 48 ÷ 8 = (6) x 6 = (36)

Bonus

54
÷
6
[9]
x
4
[36]
÷
9
[4]

© 1996 Kelley Wingate Publications   66   KW 1303

Name _____ Skill: Multiplication/Division

Leapfrog
Use your math facts to move across the lily pads.

1. 100 ÷ 10 = (10) x 9 = (90)
2. 9 x 8 = (72) ÷ 12 = (6)
3. 5 x 12 = (60) ÷ 10 = (6)
4. 63 ÷ 9 = (7) x 7 = (49)
5. 6 x 6 = (36) ÷ 9 = (4)
6. 81 ÷ 9 = (9) x 12 = (108)
7. 132 ÷ 11 = (12) x 6 = (72)
8. 84 ÷ 7 = (12) x 3 = (36)
9. 108 ÷ 12 = (9) x 3 = (27)
10. 12 x 4 = (48) ÷ 6 = (8)

Bonus

5
x
2
[10]
x
4
[40]
÷
1
[40]

© 1996 Kelley Wingate Publications   67   KW 1303

Name _____ Skill: Multiplication/Division

Leapfrog
Use your math facts to move across the lily pads.

1. 144 ÷ 12 = (12) x 8 = (96)
2. 6 x 12 = (72) ÷ 9 = (8)
3. 132 ÷ 12 = (11) x 5 = (55)
4. 5 x 8 = (40) ÷ 10 = (4)
5. 81 ÷ 9 = (9) x 8 = (72)
6. 3 x 12 = (36) ÷ 4 = (9)
7. 110 ÷ 11 = (10) x 3 = (30)
8. 44 ÷ 4 = (11) x 12 = (132)
9. 12 x 5 = (60) ÷ 10 = (6)
10. 4 x 12 = (48) ÷ 8 = (6)

Bonus

120
÷
10
[12]
÷
4
[3]
x
9
[27]

© 1996 Kelley Wingate Publications   68   KW 1303

Answer Key

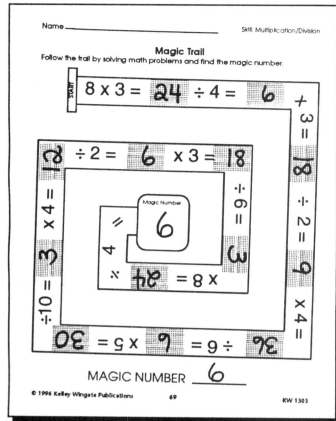

Name _____   Skill: Multiplication/Division

Magic Trail
Follow the trail by solving math problems and find the magic number.

START | 8 × 3 = **24** ÷ 4 = **6**

Magic Number **6**

MAGIC NUMBER **6**

© 1996 Kelley Wingate Publications   69   KW 1303

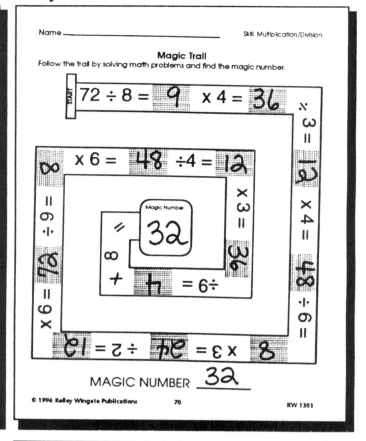

Name _____   Skill: Multiplication/Division

Magic Trail
Follow the trail by solving math problems and find the magic number.

START | 72 ÷ 8 = **9**   × 4 = **36**

Magic Number **32**

MAGIC NUMBER **32**

© 1996 Kelley Wingate Publications   70   KW 1303

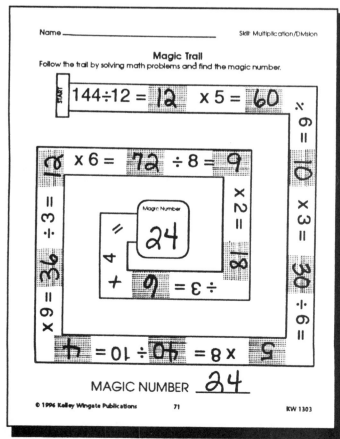

Name _____   Skill: Multiplication/Division

Magic Trail
Follow the trail by solving math problems and find the magic number.

START | 144 ÷ 12 = **12**   × 5 = **60**

Magic Number **24**

MAGIC NUMBER **24**

© 1996 Kelley Wingate Publications   71   KW 1303

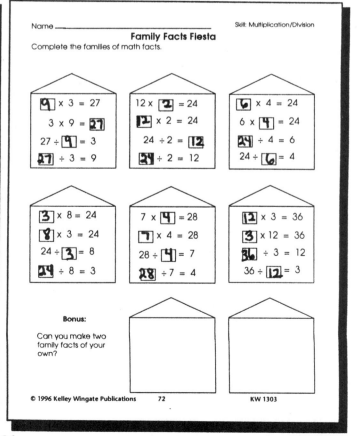

Name _____   Skill: Multiplication/Division

Family Facts Fiesta
Complete the families of math facts.

9 × 3 = 27
3 × 9 = **27**
27 ÷ **9** = 3
27 ÷ 3 = 9

12 × **2** = 24
12 × 2 = 24
24 ÷ 2 = **12**
24 ÷ 2 = 12

6 × 4 = 24
6 × **4** = 24
24 ÷ 4 = 6
24 ÷ **6** = 4

3 × 8 = 24
8 × 3 = 24
24 ÷ **3** = 8
24 ÷ 8 = 3

7 × **4** = 28
7 × 4 = 28
28 ÷ **4** = 7
28 ÷ 7 = 4

12 × 3 = 36
3 × 12 = 36
36 ÷ 3 = 12
36 ÷ **12** = 3

Bonus:
Can you make two family facts of your own?

© 1996 Kelley Wingate Publications   72   KW 1303

© 1996 Kelley Wingate Publications   121   CD-3723

Answer Key

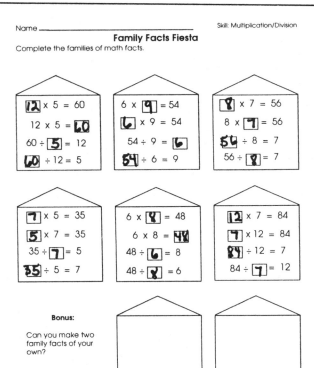

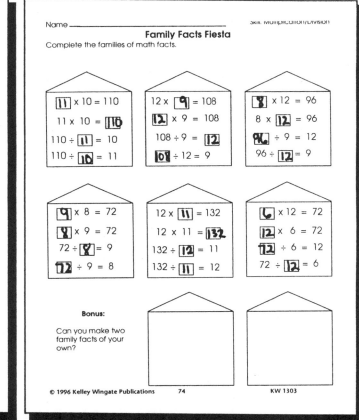

Family Facts Fiesta (page 73)

Name _____ Skill: Multiplication/Division

Family Facts Fiesta
Complete the families of math facts.

12 x 5 = 60	6 x **9** = 54	**8** x 7 = 56
12 x 5 = **60**	**6** x 9 = 54	8 x **7** = 56
60 ÷ **5** = 12	54 ÷ 9 = **6**	**56** ÷ 8 = 7
60 ÷ 12 = 5	**54** ÷ 6 = 9	56 ÷ **8** = 7

7 x 5 = 35	6 x **8** = 48	**12** x 7 = 84
5 x 7 = 35	6 x 8 = **48**	**7** x 12 = 84
35 ÷ **7** = 5	48 ÷ **6** = 8	**84** ÷ 12 = 7
35 ÷ 5 = 7	48 ÷ **8** = 6	84 ÷ **7** = 12

Bonus:
Can you make two family facts of your own?

© 1996 Kelley Wingate Publications   73   KW 1303

Family Facts Fiesta (page 74)

Name _____ Skill: Multiplication/Division

Family Facts Fiesta
Complete the families of math facts.

11 x 10 = 110	12 x **9** = 108	**8** x 12 = 96
11 x 10 = **110**	**12** x 9 = 108	8 x **12** = 96
110 ÷ **11** = 10	108 ÷ 9 = **12**	**96** ÷ 9 = 12
110 ÷ **10** = 11	**108** ÷ 12 = 9	96 ÷ **12** = 9

9 x 8 = 72	12 x **11** = 132	**6** x 12 = 72
8 x 9 = 72	12 x 11 = **132**	**12** x 6 = 72
72 ÷ **8** = 9	132 ÷ **12** = 11	**72** ÷ 6 = 12
72 ÷ 9 = 8	132 ÷ **11** = 12	72 ÷ **12** = 6

Bonus:
Can you make two family facts of your own?

© 1996 Kelley Wingate Publications   74   KW 1303

Mystery Math (page 75)

Name _____ Skill: Multiplication/Division

Mystery Math
Look at the mystery number. Circle all math expressions in that row wich equal the mystery number. The first problem is done for you.

Mystery Number	Math Expression			
6	35 ÷ 7	(12 ÷ 2)	(18 ÷ 3)	(2 x 3)
7	64 ÷ 8	(56 ÷ 8)	27 ÷ 3	32 ÷ 4
5	42 ÷ 6	(60 ÷ 12)	35 ÷ 5	(25 ÷ 5)
12	(96 ÷ 8)	4 x 4	(144 ÷ 12)	(3 x 4)
24	(4 x 6)	(3 x 8)	120 ÷ 12	10 x 4
9	(63 ÷ 7)	(3 x 3)	72 ÷ 9	(81 ÷ 9)
11	6 x 2	(44 ÷ 4)	(121 ÷ 11)	120 ÷ 10
12	72 ÷ 8	60 ÷ 6	(3 x 4)	(48 ÷ 4)
10	2 x 6	(100 ÷ 10)	(2 x 5)	120 ÷ 10

© 1996 Kelley Wingate Publications   75   KW 1303

Mystery Math (page 76)

Name _____ Skill: Multiplication/Division

Mystery Math
Look at the mystery number. Circle all math expressions in that row wich equal the mystery number. The first problem is done for you.

Mystery Number	Math Expression			
3	12 ÷ 6	2 x 4	(15 ÷ 5)	(21 ÷ 7)
11	4 x 7	(77 ÷ 7)	30 ÷ 3	(132 ÷ 12)
5	(60 ÷ 12)	4 x 2	(55 ÷ 11)	28 ÷ 7
12	(6 x 2)	(132 ÷ 11)	60 ÷ 6	4 x 4
9	80 ÷ 8	(3 x 3)	(81 ÷ 9)	(72 ÷ 8)
7	(28 ÷ 4)	(49 ÷ 7)	3 x 2	27 ÷ 3
10	60 ÷ 10	(2 x 5)	45 ÷ 5	(110 ÷ 11)
12	(60 ÷ 5)	(3 x 4)	(12 x 1)	(120 ÷ 10)
8	24 ÷ 4	3 x 5	(32 ÷ 4)	8 x 0

© 1996 Kelley Wingate Publications   76   KW 1303

Answer Key

Name _____ Skill: Multiplication/Division

MISSING FACTORS
Solve the problems by filling in the box with a number that will make the math statement true.

1. [12] ÷ 6 = 2
2. [18] ÷ 3 = 6
3. [40] ÷ 5 = 8
4. [20] ÷ 4 = 5
5. [36] ÷ 6 = 6
6. [45] ÷ 9 = 5
7. [21] ÷ 7 = 3
8. [36] ÷ 3 = 12
9. [42] ÷ 6 = 7
10. [32] ÷ 8 = 4
11. [24] ÷ 2 = 12
12. [35] ÷ 7 = 5
13. [27] ÷ 9 = 3
14. [10] ÷ 5 = 2
15. [48] ÷ 6 = 8
16. [25] ÷ 5 = 5
17. [36] ÷ 6 = 6
18. [28] ÷ 7 = 4
19. [54] ÷ 6 = 9
20. [24] ÷ 3 = 8
21. [40] ÷ 4 = 10
22. [36] ÷ 9 = 4
23. [36] ÷ 3 = 12
24. [15] ÷ 5 = 3
25. [56] ÷ 7 = 8
26. [40] ÷ 4 = 10
27. [36] ÷ 9 = 4
28. [16] ÷ 2 = 8
29. [40] ÷ 5 = 8
30. [14] ÷ 7 = 2

© 1996 Kelley Wingate Publications   77   KW 1303

MISSING FACTORS
Solve the problems by filling in the box with a number that will make the math statement true.

1. [70] ÷ 7 = 10
2. [48] ÷ 6 = 8
3. [120] ÷ 12 = 10
4. [54] ÷ 6 = 9
5. [48] ÷ 8 = 6
6. [96] ÷ 8 = 12
7. [63] ÷ 9 = 7
8. [36] ÷ 4 = 9
9. [64] ÷ 8 = 8
10. [100] ÷ 10 = 10
11. [21] ÷ 7 = 3
12. [108] ÷ 9 = 12
13. [56] ÷ 7 = 8
14. [40] ÷ 8 = 5
15. [110] ÷ 10 = 11
16. [77] ÷ 11 = 7
17. [42] ÷ 7 = 6
18. [108] ÷ 12 = 9
19. [81] ÷ 9 = 9
20. [84] ÷ 7 = 12
21. [72] ÷ 9 = 8
22. [121] ÷ 11 = 11
23. [49] ÷ 7 = 7
24. [40] ÷ 5 = 8
25. [90] ÷ 10 = 9
26. [48] ÷ 4 = 12
27. [81] ÷ 9 = 9
28. [72] ÷ 12 = 6
29. [40] ÷ 5 = 8
30. [18] ÷ 9 = 2

© 1996 Kelley Wingate Publications   78   KW 1303

MISSING FACTORS
Solve the problems by filling in the box with a number that will make the math statement true.

1. [32] ÷ 4 = 8
2. [54] ÷ 9 = 6
3. [64] ÷ 8 = 8
4. [55] ÷ 11 = 5
5. [56] ÷ 8 = 7
6. [72] ÷ 9 = 8
7. [110] ÷ 10 = 11
8. [132] ÷ 12 = 11
9. [84] ÷ 7 = 12
10. [121] ÷ 11 = 11
11. [108] ÷ 12 = 9
12. [88] ÷ 8 = 11
13. [48] ÷ 8 = 6
14. [120] ÷ 10 = 12
15. [48] ÷ 12 = 4
16. [132] ÷ 11 = 12
17. [54] ÷ 9 = 6
18. [27] ÷ 3 = 9
19. [63] ÷ 9 = 7
20. [144] ÷ 12 = 12
21. [44] ÷ 4 = 11
22. [81] ÷ 9 = 9
23. [100] ÷ 10 = 10
24. [15] ÷ 5 = 3
25. [90] ÷ 9 = 10
26. [60] ÷ 5 = 12
27. [77] ÷ 7 = 11
28. [30] ÷ 10 = 3
29. [50] ÷ 5 = 10
30. [63] ÷ 7 = 9

© 1996 Kelley Wingate Publications   79   KW 1303

MISSING FACTORS
Solve the problems by filling in the box with a number that will make the math statement true.

1. [16] ÷ 4 = 4
2. [24] ÷ 4 = 6
3. [99] ÷ 9 = 11
4. [35] ÷ 5 = 7
5. [25] ÷ 5 = 5
6. [132] ÷ 12 = 11
7. [54] ÷ 9 = 6
8. [24] ÷ 8 = 3
9. [108] ÷ 12 = 9
10. [36] ÷ 6 = 6
11. [144] ÷ 12 = 12
12. [24] ÷ 12 = 2
13. [30] ÷ 3 = 10
14. [42] ÷ 7 = 6
15. [121] ÷ 11 = 11
16. [56] ÷ 7 = 8
17. [45] ÷ 9 = 5
18. [32] ÷ 8 = 4
19. [63] ÷ 7 = 9
20. [48] ÷ 12 = 4
21. [72] ÷ 9 = 8
22. [72] ÷ 12 = 6
23. [96] ÷ 8 = 12
24. [55] ÷ 5 = 11
25. [32] ÷ 4 = 8
26. [80] ÷ 8 = 10
27. [77] ÷ 7 = 11
28. [60] ÷ 12 = 5
29. [88] ÷ 11 = 8
30. [70] ÷ 7 = 10

© 1996 Kelley Wingate Publications   80   KW 1303

Answer Key

Worksheet 1 (Page 81)

Name _____

Place Space

Skill: Place Value

Hundred Thousands	Ten Thousands	One Thousand	Hundreds	Tens	Ones	Tenths	Hundredths
9	3	2 ,	4	8	6 .	1	7

1. Name the place value of the digit "4" in these numbers:

A. 3,432 __hundreds__ B. 42,351 __tenthousands__
C. 45 __tens__ D. 473,115 __hundred thousands__
E. 620.48 __tenths__ F. 504.3 __ones__
G. 81.34 __hundredths__ H. 64,332.5 __thousands__
I. 888,415 __hundreds__ J. 74.3 __ones__

2. Tell which digit is in the tens place:

A. 1,536 __3__ B. 53 __5__
C. 47.2 __4__ D. 504.6 __0__
E. 8,346 __4__ F. 416.8 __1__
G. 902 __0__ H. 52,374 __7__
I. 357,618 __1__ J. 495 __9__

3. Tell which digit is in the tenths place:

A. 15.25 __2__ B. 1.9 __9__
C. 325.17 __1__ D. 516.87 __8__
E. 45.8 __8__ F. 24.3 __3__
G. 6.27 __2__ H. 742.16 __1__
I. 534.06 __0__ J. 9,834.12 __1__

© 1996 Kelley Wingate Publications 81 KW 1303

Worksheet 2 (Page 82)

Name _____

Place Space

Skill: Place Value

Hundred Thousands	Ten Thousands	One Thousand	Hundreds	Tens	Ones	Tenths	Hundredths
4	5	9 ,	3	6	7 .	1	2

1. Name the place value of the digit "9" in these numbers:

A. 309 __ones__ B. 17,059 __ones__
C. 159,342 __thousands__ D. 475,912 __hundreds__
E. 92,105 __ten thousands__ F. 8.49 __hundredths__
G. 962 __hundreds__ H. 142.95 __tenths__
I. 5,896 __tens__ J. 9,178 __thousands__

2. Tell which digit is in the ones place:

A. 342 __2__ B. 126 __6__
C. 4,715 __5__ D. 54,781 __1__
E. 56,783 __3__ F. 1,342.7 __2__
G. 310.26 __0__ H. 10.59 __0__
I. 79 __9__ J. 843.2 __3__

3. Tell which digit is in the hundreds place:

A. 852 __8__ B. 46,283 __2__
C. 3,946.5 __9__ D. 3,542.1 __5__
E. 81,407 __4__ F. 123,748 __7__
G. 9,364.17 __3__ H. 675 __6__
I. 345,120 __1__ J. 3,412.05 __4__

© 1996 Kelley Wingate Publications 82 KW 1303

Worksheet 3 (Page 83)

Name _____

Rounding Round-Up

Skill: Rounding Numbers

To round any number, follow these simple rules:
Underline the place value you are rounding to.
Circle the digit to the right of the underlined digit.
If the circled number is 0, 1, 2, 3, or 4 the underlined digit stays the same.
If the circled number is 5, 6, 7, 8, or 9 the underlined digit goes up by 1.
The circled digit and all digits to the right become a zero.

1. Round these numbers to the nearest ten:

A. 42 __40__ B. 554 __550__
C. 87 __90__ D. 436 __440__
E. 133 __130__ F. 3,771 __3,770__
G. 289 __290__ H. 408 __410__
I. 1,415 __1,420__ J. 1,982 __1,980__

2. Round these numbers to the nearest hundred:

A. 3,288 __3,300__ B. 551 __600__
C. 768 __800__ D. 381 __400__
E. 1,349 __1,300__ F. 675 __700__
G. 156 __200__ H. 7,245 __7,200__
I. 8,337 __8,300__ J. 2,819 __2,800__

3. Round these numbers to the nearest thousand:

A. 4,670 __5,000__ B. 46,667 __47,000__
C. 3,099 __3,000__ D. 3,501 __4,000__
E. 61,389 __61,000__ F. 23,748 __24,000__
G. 9,364 __9,000__ H. 2,651 __3,000__
I. 215,189 __215,000__ J. 3,712 __4,000__

© 1996 Kelley Wingate Publications 83 KW 1303

Worksheet 4 (Page 84)

Name _____

Rounding Round-Up

Skill: Rounding Numbers

To round any number, follow these simple rules:
Underline the place value you are rounding to.
Circle the digit to the right of the underlined digit.
If the circled number is 0, 1, 2, 3, or 4 the underlined digit stays the same.
If the circled number is 5, 6, 7, 8, or 9 the underlined digit goes up by 1.
The circled digit and all digits to the right become a zero.

1. Round these numbers to the nearest hundred:

A. 646 __600__ B. 867 __900__
C. 172 __200__ D. 759 __800__
E. 345 __300__ F. 3,498 __3,500__
G. 581 __600__ H. 735 __700__
I. 1,293 __1,300__ J. 1,611 __1,600__

2. Round these numbers to the nearest thousand:

A. 3,397 __3,000__ B. 5,551 __6,000__
C. 1,768 __2,000__ D. 8,381 __8,000__
E. 4,349 __4,000__ F. 12,675 __13,000__
G. 7,156 __7,000__ H. 7,245 __7,000__
I. 18,337 __18,000__ J. 2,719 __3,000__

3. Round these numbers to the nearest tenth:

A. 12.84 __12.8__ B. 176.94 __176.9__
C. 304.46 __304.5__ D. 22.38 __22.4__
E. 88.13 __88.1__ F. 5.26 __5.3__
G. 749.82 __749.8__ H. 36.76 __36.8__
I. 8.57 __8.6__ J. 9.31 __9.3__

© 1996 Kelley Wingate Publications 84 KW 1303

Answer Key

Worksheet 1

Name _____

Rounding Round-Up

To round any number, follow these simple rules:
Underline the place value you are rounding to.
Circle the digit to the right of the underlined digit.
If the circled number is 0, 1, 2, 3, or 4 the underlined digit stays the same.
If the circled number is 5, 6, 7, 8, or 9 the underlined digit goes up by 1.
The circled digit and all digits to the right become a zero.

1. Round these numbers to the nearest hundred:

   A. 1,442 __1,400__   B. 426 __400__
   C. 839 __800__   D. 854 __900__
   E. 4,562 __4,600__   F. 3,396 __3,400__
   G. 339 __300__   H. 40,491 __40,500__
   I. 881 __900__   J. 1,816 __1,800__

2. Round these numbers to the nearest thousand:

   A. 38,815 __39,000__   B. 6,587 __7,000__
   C. 5,446 __5,000__   D. 14,318 __14,000__
   E. 7,227 __7,000__   F. 5,672 __6,000__
   G. 4,980 __5,000__   H. 9,194 __9,000__
   I. 11,392 __11,000__   J. 43,488 __43,000__

3. Round these numbers to the nearest ten thousand:

   A. 24,170 __20,000__   B. 47,127 __50,000__
   C. 55,099 __60,000__   D. 83,591 __80,000__
   E. 62,989 __60,000__   F. 26,748 __30,000__
   G. 19,764 __20,000__   H. 92,651 __90,000__
   I. 217,105 __220,000__   J. 138,712 __140,000__

Worksheet 2

Name _____

Decimal Dimensions

A. Write each fraction as a decimal:

1. $\frac{32}{100}$ 0.32   6. $\frac{5}{10}$ 0.5
2. $\frac{9}{10}$ 0.9   7. $\frac{23}{100}$ 0.23
3. $\frac{48}{100}$ 0.48   8. $\frac{6}{100}$ 0.06
4. $\frac{7}{100}$ 0.07   9. $\frac{95}{100}$ 0.95
5. $\frac{1}{10}$ 0.1   10. $\frac{14}{100}$ 0.14

B. Write each decimal as a fraction:

1. 0.5 $\frac{5}{10}$ 6. 0.8 $\frac{8}{10}$
2. 0.31 $\frac{31}{100}$ 7. 0.3 $\frac{3}{10}$
3. 0.48 $\frac{48}{100}$ 8. 0.24 $\frac{24}{100}$
4. 0.4 $\frac{4}{10}$ 9. 0.7 $\frac{7}{10}$
5. 0.08 $\frac{8}{100}$ 10. 0.56 $\frac{56}{100}$

C. Write each expression as a fraction and a decimal:

1. six tenths $\frac{6}{10}$, 0.6
2. four hundredths $\frac{4}{100}$, 0.04

Worksheet 3

Name _____

Decimal Dimensions

A. Write each mixed number as a decimal:

$5\frac{6}{10}$ 5.6 $7\frac{8}{10}$ 7.8

$42\frac{3}{100}$ 42.03 $13\frac{13}{100}$ 13.13

$71\frac{3}{10}$ 71.3 $5\frac{81}{100}$ 5.81

$4\frac{8}{100}$ 4.08 $14\frac{2}{100}$ 14.02

$1\frac{1}{100}$ 1.01 $3\frac{3}{10}$ 3.3

B. Write each decimal as a fraction:

1. 3.52 $3\frac{52}{100}$ 6. 4.09 $4\frac{9}{100}$
2. 27.09 $27\frac{9}{100}$ 7. 70.2 $70\frac{2}{10}$
3. 5.1 $5\frac{1}{10}$ 8. 12.17 $12\frac{17}{100}$
4. 30.25 $30\frac{25}{100}$ 9. 5.18 $5\frac{18}{100}$
5. 12.04 $12\frac{4}{100}$ 10. 1.4 $1\frac{4}{10}$

C. Write each expression as a fraction and a decimal:

1. seven and one tenth $7\frac{1}{10}$, 7.1
2. ninety and four hundredth $90\frac{4}{100}$, 90.04

Worksheet 4

Name _____

What Is Next?

Find the pattern in each series below. Write the next three members of the series on the lines. Write the pattern rule (+ or - and number).

1. 5, 10, 15, 20, 25, 30, __35 40 45__
   Rule: + 5

2. 18, 16, 14, 12, 10, __8 6 4__
   Rule: - 2

3. 3, 6, 9, 12, 15, __18 21 24__
   Rule: + 3

4. 100, 94, 88, 82, 76, __70 64 58__
   Rule: - 6

5. 240, 250, 260, 270, 280, __290 300 310__
   Rule: + 10

6. 3,500, 3,400, 3,300, 3,200, __3,100 3,000 2,900__
   Rule: - 100

7. 12, 24, 36, 48, 60, 72, __84 96 108__
   Rule: + 12

8. 80, 72, 64, 56, 48, 40, __32 24 16__
   Rule: - 8

9. 11, 22, 33, 44, 55, 66, __77 88 99__
   Rule: + 11

10. 4, 8, 12, 16, 20, 24, __28 32 36__
    Rule: + 4

Bonus: Design your own pattern for your class to solve.

Answer Key

What Is Next?

Name _____

Skill: Patterns

Find the pattern in each series below. Write the next three members of the series on the lines. Write the pattern rule (+ or - and number).

1. 5, 10, 15, 20, 25, 30, **35 40 45**
   Rule: **+ 5**

2. 111, 112, 113, 114, 115, **116 117 118**
   Rule: **+ 1**

3. 125, 120, 115, 110, 105, **100 95 90**
   Rule: **- 5**

4. 28, 35, 42, 49, 56, **63 70 77**
   Rule: **+ 7**

5. 12, 23, 34, 45, 56, **67 78 89**
   Rule: **+ 11**

6. 78, 75, 72, 69, 66, **63 60 57**
   Rule: **- 3**

7. 1,300, 1,250, 1,200, 1,150, **1,100 1,050 1,000**
   Rule: **- 50**

8. 88, 98, 108, 118, 128, **138 148 158**
   Rule: **+ 10**

9. 10, 25, 40, 55, 70, 85, **100 115 130**
   Rule: **+ 15**

10. 210, 180, 150, 120, 90, **60 30 0**
    Rule: **- 30**

Bonus: Design your own pattern for your class to solve.

© 1996 Kelley Wingate Publications   89   KW 1303

Picture Perfect

Name _____

Skill: Fractions

Look at the pictures below. Shade in the parts to show the fraction named. Remember, the number of shaded parts goes on the top and the total number of parts goes on the bottom.

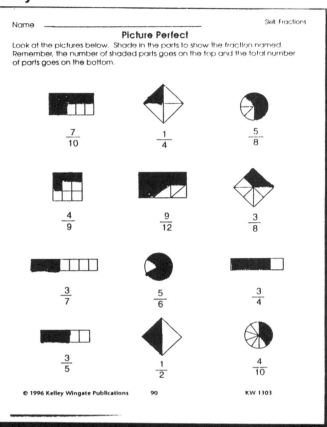

© 1996 Kelley Wingate Publications   90   KW 1303

Picture Perfect

Name _____

Skill: Fractions

Look at the fractions in each pair. Name the equal fractions.

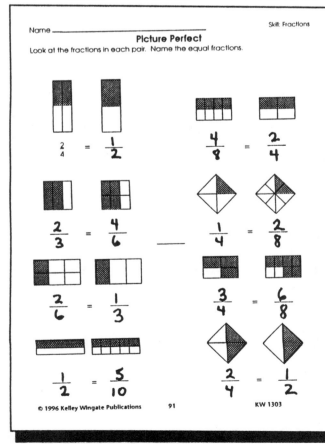

© 1996 Kelley Wingate Publications   91   KW 1303

Compare Squares

Name _____

Skill: Fractions

Write a fraction to name the shaded parts for each figure. Write >, <, or = for each pair.

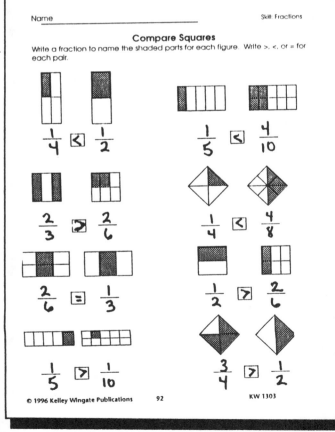

© 1996 Kelley Wingate Publications   92   KW 1303

Answer Key

Page 93

Name_____

Skill: Geometry

Perimeter

Find the perimeter of each shape by adding the measurement of each side.

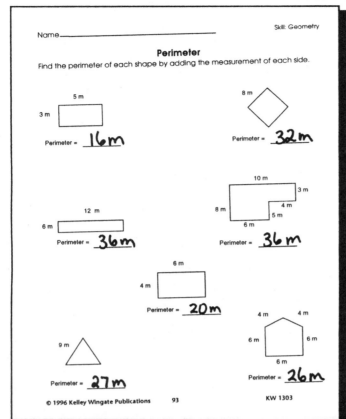

Perimeter = __16m__

Perimeter = __32m__

Perimeter = __36m__

Perimeter = __36m__

Perimeter = __20m__

Perimeter = __27m__

Perimeter = __26m__

© 1996 Kelley Wingate Publications   93   KW 1303

Page 94

Name_____

Skill: Word Problems

Words Into Math

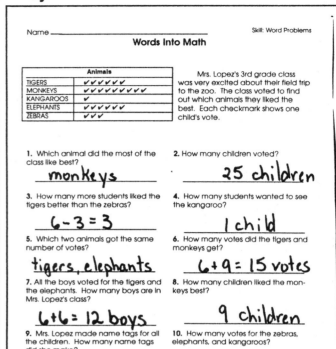

Animals	
TIGERS	✓✓✓✓✓✓
MONKEYS	✓✓✓✓✓✓✓✓✓
KANGAROOS	✓
ELEPHANTS	✓✓✓✓✓✓
ZEBRAS	✓✓✓

Mrs. Lopez's 3rd grade class was very excited about their field trip to the zoo. The class voted to find out which animals they liked the best. Each checkmark shows one child's vote.

1. Which animal did the most of the class like best?

__monkeys__

2. How many children voted?

__25 children__

3. How many more students liked the tigers better than the zebras?

__6 - 3 = 3__

4. How many students wanted to see the kangaroo?

__1 child__

5. Which two animals got the same number of votes?

__tigers, elephants__

6. How many votes did the tigers and monkeys get?

__6 + 9 = 15 votes__

7. All the boys voted for the tigers and the elephants. How many boys are in Mrs. Lopez's class?

__6 + 6 = 12 boys__

8. How many children liked the monkeys best?

__9 children__

9. Mrs. Lopez made name tags for all the children. How many name tags did she make?

__25 tags__

10. How many votes for the zebras, elephants, and kangaroos?

__3 + 6 + 1 = 10 votes__

© 1996 Kelley Wingate Publications   94   KW 1303

Page 95

Name_____

Skill: Word Problems

Words Into Math

ACTIVITY	STARTING TIME
Band Practice	2:45 PM
Football Practice	3:00 PM
Cheerleading Practice	2:45 PM
Ecology Club Meeting	2:40 PM
Honors Club Meeting	2:50 PM
Chorus Practice	3:30 PM

City State High School has this schedule posted. It names all of the after school activities for clubs and sports groups. It also gives the time each one starts.

1. What time does cheerleading practice begin?

__2:45 P.M.__

2. What time does band practice begin?

__2:45 P.M.__

3. Which two activities start at the same time?

__band, cheerleading__

4. Football begins at 3:00. How much later before chorus begins?

__30 mins. later__

5. How many minutes between the time band and football practice starts?

__15 mins.__

6. Chorus practice ends at 5:00. How long is practice?

__1½ hours__

7. Which starts earlier, Honors Club or band practice?

__band__

8. Football practice ends at 5 PM. How long does practice last?

__2 hours__

9. Matt was 10 minutes late for Honors Club. What time did he get there?

__3:00 P.M.__

10. Can Joe go to band practice and the ecology club meeting?

__No__

© 1996 Kelley Wingate Publications   95   KW 1303

Page 96

Name_____

Skill: Word Problems

Words Into Math

FOOD	VOTES
Tacos	★★★
Chicken Nuggets	★★★★★
Pizza	★★★★★★★
Hot Dog	★★★★
Hamburger	★★★★★
Spaghetti	★★★★★★

One day each week a class at school votes on what food will be served on "free day". This week the third graders voted. This chart shows how they voted. Each star stands for five votes.

1. How many children voted for tacos on free day?

__15 children__

2. Which food got the most votes for free day?

__Pizza__

3. How many children voted for spaghetti?

__30 children__

4. Did more children vote for hot dogs or hamburgers?

__hamburgers__

5. Which two foods got the same number of votes?

__chicken nuggets, hamburger__

6. How many votes did pizza get?

__35 votes__

7. Which food got 20 votes?

__hot dogs__

8. Which food got the fewest votes?

__tacos__

9. How many students voted this week?

__150 students__

10. How many students voted for chicken, pizza, and tacos all together?

__25 + 35 + 15 = 75 students__

© 1996 Kelley Wingate Publications   96   KW 1303

Answer Key

Skill: Word Problems

Words Into Math

MENU	
Cheeseburger	$2.00
Hamburger	$1.90
French Fries	$ .85
Soda	$ .70
Milk Shake	$1.25
Ice Cream	$ .95

Mr. Smith's third grade class stopped at Burger Bonanza to eat lunch during their field trip last week. This is the menu the children had to choose from.

1. How much does a milk shake cost?

$1.25

2. What item costs more than anything else on the menu?

cheeseburger

3. How much more does a cheese-burger cost than a hamburger?

$2.00 - $1.90 = $.10

4. Which costs more, a milk shake or hamburger?

hamburger

5. How much does french fries and a soda cost all together?

.85 + .70 = $1.55

6. Chris ate his lunch and he had 80¢ left. Could he buy anything else?

yes - a soda

7. How much does a hamburger, fries, and ice cream cost?

1.90 + .85 + .95 = $3.70

8. Lisa ordered a hamburger and a milk shake. How much did she spend?

1.90 + 1.25 = $3.15

9. Hallie had $5.00. Could she buy a cheeseburger, fries, and a milk shake?

yes

10. Shelia has $3.00. Can she buy a cheeseburger and milk shake?

no

97 KW 1303

Skill: Word Problems

Words Into Math
Read the paragraph carefully then answer the questions.

There are some really good players on Jamal's Little League baseball team. For the first five games, Sam got 11 hits. Javier got 9 hits. Charlie has had 4 hits. There are still 3 games left to play this season.

1. How many hits have Javier and Sam gotten together?

9 + 11 = 20 hits

2. Who got more hits, Charlie or Javier?

Javier

3. Jamal got three times as many hits as Javier. How many hits did Jamal get?

3 × 9 = 27 hits

4. How many games will the boys play this season?

5 + 3 = 8 games

5. Who got more hits, Sam or Charlie?

Sam

6. How many hits have Javier, Sam, and Charlie gotten all together?

9 + 11 + 4 = 24 hits

7. Charlie had 8 hits less than Greg. How many hits did Greg get?

4 + 8 = 12 hits

8. How many hits did Javier and Charlie get together?

9 + 4 = 13 hits

98 KW 1303

Skill: Review

Skills Evaluation
Choose the best answer to these review questions.
Circle the correct answer.

1. Add: 3,442
+ 4,258

A. 7,690 B. 7,600

C. 6,700 **D. 7,700**

2. Subtract: 1,862
- 785

A. 1,123 **B. 1,077**

C. 1,177 D. 1,083

3. Subtract: 5,040
- 3,639

A. 2,619 B. 1,301

C. 1,419 **D. 1,401**

4. Multiply: 12 x 11

A. 121 B. 120

C. 132 D. 123

5. Which of these facts is not correct?

A. 6 x 9 = 54 **B. 12 x 10 = 121**

C. 9 x 7 = 63 D. 5 x 8 = 40

6. Which problem does not have a product of 24?

A. 12 x 2 B. 3 x 8

C. 4 x 5 D. 6 x 4

7. Which of the multiplication facts is correct?

A. 11 x 10 = 111 **B. 12 x 7 = 84**

C. 7 x 8 = 54 D. 8 x 8 = 81

8. Solve: 4 x 9 + 6 = ☐

A. 12 B. 36

C. 6 D. 8

9. Find the missing factor:
27 ÷ ☐ = 9

A. 4 **B. 3**

C. 7 D. 2

10. Find the missing factor:
72 ÷ ☐ = 8

A. 12 B. 7

C. 8 **D. 9**

99 KW 1303

Skill: Review

Skills Evaluation
Choose the best answer to these review questions.
Circle the correct answer.

1. Find the missing factor:
96 ÷ ☐ = 12

A. 7 **B. 8**

C. 9 D. 10

2. Find the missing factor:
55 ÷ ☐ = 5

A. 8 B. 9

C. 10 **D. 11**

3. The number is 157,236. The 3 is in which place?

A. ones **B. tens**

C. hundreds D. thousands

4. The number is 30,521. The 3 is in which place?

A. tens B. hundreds

C. thousands **D. ten thousands**

5. The number is 13,987. The 3 is in which place?

A. ones B. tens

C. hundreds **D. thousands**

6. The number is 25,376. The 3 is in which place?

A. tens **B. hundreds**

C. thousands D. ten thousands

7. Round to the nearest ten:
461

A. 462 **B. 460**

C. 470 D. 500

8. Round to the nearest hundred:
1,548

A. 1,550 B. 1,540

C. 1,500 D. 1,600

9. Round to the nearest hundred:
691

A. 1,000 B. 690

C. 680 **D. 700**

10. Round to the nearest thousand:
15,820

A. 15,000 B. 15,800

C. 15,900 **D. 16,000**

100 KW 1303

Answer Key

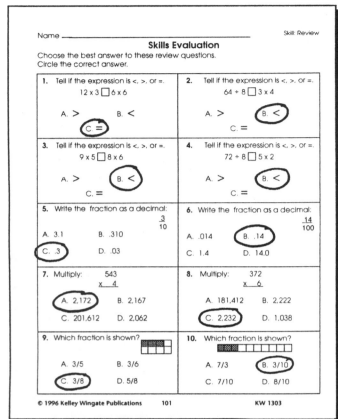

Name _____

Skill: Review

Skills Evaluation

Choose the best answer to these review questions.
Circle the correct answer.

1. Tell if the expression is <, >, or =.

$12 \times 3 \square 6 \times 6$

A. >   B. <

C. =

2. Tell if the expression is <, >, or =.

$64 \div 8 \square 3 \times 4$

A. >   B. <

C. =

3. Tell if the expression is <, >, or =.

$9 \times 5 \square 8 \times 6$

A. >   B. <

C. =

4. Tell if the expression is <, >, or =.

$72 \div 8 \square 5 \times 2$

A. >   B. <

C. =

5. Write the fraction as a decimal:

$\frac{3}{10}$

A. 3.1   B. .310

C. .3   D. .03

6. Write the fraction as a decimal:

$\frac{14}{100}$

A. .014   B. .14

C. 1.4   D. 14.0

7. Multiply: 543
$\underline{\times\ 4}$

A. 2,172   B. 2,167

C. 201,612   D. 2,062

8. Multiply: 372
$\underline{\times\ 6}$

A. 181,412   B. 2,222

C. 2,232   D. 1,038

9. Which fraction is shown?

A. 3/5   B. 3/6

C. 3/8   D. 5/8

10. Which fraction is shown?

A. 7/3   B. 3/10

C. 7/10   D. 8/10

Great Success!

_____ earns this award for

I am Proud of You!

_____ Signed

_____ Date

CD-3723

You Did It!

earns this award for _____

Keep Up The Great Work!

Signed _____

Date _____

Keep up the Great Work!

_____

earns this award for

You are TERRIFIC!

Signed

Date

Certificate of Completion

This certificate certifies that

Has completed

Signed

Date

CD-3723

You Did It!

_____

earns this award for

_____

Keep Up The Great Work!

_____ _____
Signed   Date

Great Success!

earns this award for

_____

I am Proud of You!

Signed _____

Date _____

1 x 1	1 x 2	1 x 3	1 x 4
1 x 5	1 x 6	1 x 7	1 x 8
1 x 9	10 x 1	12 x 1	2 x 2
2 x 3	2 x 4	2 x 5	2 x 6

4	3	2	1
8	7	6	5
4	12	10	9
12	10	8	6

2 x 7	2 x 8	2 x 9	10 x 2
11 x 2	12 x 2	3 x 3	3 x 4
3 x 5	3 x 6	3 x 7	3 x 8
3 x 9	10 x 3	11 x 3	12 x 3

20	18	16	14
12	9	24	22
24	21	18	15
36	33	30	27

$3\overline{)12}$	$2\overline{)12}$	$5\overline{)10}$	$2\overline{)10}$
$9\overline{)9}$	$3\overline{)9}$	$4\overline{)8}$	$2\overline{)8}$
$6\overline{)6}$	$3\overline{)6}$	$2\overline{)6}$	$5\overline{)5}$
$4\overline{)4}$	$2\overline{)4}$	$3\overline{)3}$	$2\overline{)2}$

5	2	6	4
4	2	3	1
1	3	2	1
1	1	2	1

10 x 8	11 x 8	12 x 8	9 x 9
10 x 9	11 x 9	12 x 9	10 x 10
11 x 10	12 x 10	11 x 11	12 x 11
12 x 12	12⟌12	6⟌12	4⟌12

81 96 88 80

100 108 99 90

132 121 120 110

3 2 1 144

12 x 5	6 x 6	6 x 7	6 x 8
6 x 9	10 x 6	11 x 6	12 x 6
7 x 7	7 x 8	7 x 9	10 x 7
11 x 7	12 x 7	8 x 8	8 x 9

48 42 36 60

72 66 60 54

70 63 56 49

72 64 84 77

4 x 4	4 x 5	4 x 6	4 x 7
4 x 8	4 x 9	10 x 4	11 x 4
12 x 4	5 x 5	5 x 6	5 x 7
5 x 8	5 x 9	10 x 5	11 x 5

28	24	20	16
44	40	36	32
35	30	25	48
55	50	45	40